The Shout That Stopped The Saviour

Joshua Rhoades

Published by Joshua Paul Rhoades, 2024.

THE SHOUT THAT STOPPED THE SAVIOUR

First edition. August 31, 2024.

ISBN: 979-8227430632

Written by Joshua Rhoades.

Also by Joshua Rhoades

Courage Under Fire: David's Stand On The Battlefield
Jonah's Journey: Voices Of Redemption And Lessons In Obedience
The Furnace Of Faith: 12 Principles From The Heat Of Faith
Whispers of Hope: Inspiring Stories of Men's Prayers In Scripture
Frontier Legends: The Oregon Dream
Elijah: A Beacon Of Boldness
HOOK, LINE & SAVIOUR - Faith Reflections from Fishing
Driven By Faith: Motor Racing Inspired Christian Life
30 Day Devotional - Bold and Strong- Coffee Devotions for a Courageous Christian Walk
Authentic Christianity: The Heart of Old Time Religion
Consider The Ant - God's Tiny Preachers
Flee Fornication: The Plea For Purity
Renewed Hope- How to Find Encouragement in God
Sounding The Call - The Voice of Conviction
The Altar - Where Heaven Meets Earth
The Bible's Battlefields- Timeless Lessons from Ancient Wars
The Sacred Art of Silence - How Silence Speaks in Scripture
Under Fire- The Sanctity of the Traditional Biblical Home
Who Is on the Lord's Side? A Call to Righteousness
What Is Truth? - From Skepticism to Submission
First and Goal- Faith and Football Fundamentals
From Dugout to Devotion- Spiritual Lessons from Baseball
Par for the Course- Faith and Fairways
The Believer's Pace- Tools for Running Life's Marathon

Introduction

"The Shout That Stopped The Saviour" dives into into the remarkable story of Blind Bartimaeus, a man whose faith and desperation moved Jesus to perform one of the most memorable miracles in the Gospels. Found in Mark 10:46-52, this passage captures a moment where the cry of a blind beggar halted the steps of the Saviour, leading to a life-changing encounter. Bartimaeus' story is not just an account of physical healing; it is a profound illustration of the power of persistent faith, the significance of boldness in the face of adversity, and the deep compassion of Jesus for those who earnestly seek Him.

In the bustling city of Jericho, Bartimaeus sat by the roadside, marginalized and overlooked by society, with nothing to offer but a loud, desperate plea. When he heard that Jesus of Nazareth was passing by, he didn't hesitate. Despite the crowd's attempts to silence him, Bartimaeus cried out all the more, "Jesus, thou Son of David, have mercy on me!" This was no ordinary shout; it was a cry from the depths of his soul, a recognition of Jesus' identity as the Messiah, and a plea for mercy from the only One who could truly change his circumstances.

The power of Bartimaeus' shout lies in its unwavering faith and determination. He wasn't deterred by the rebukes of those around him. He wasn't discouraged by his lowly status or his physical blindness. Instead, he saw with the eyes of faith what others around him could not—that Jesus had the power to heal him, to restore his sight, and to transform his life. Bartimaeus' shout was an act of faith that demonstrated his belief in Jesus' ability to save, and it was this faith that stopped Jesus in His tracks.

"The Shout That Stopped The Saviour" invites readers to reflect on the nature of their own cries for help, their own expressions of faith in moments of desperation. Bartimaeus' story challenges us to consider whether we, too, are willing to cry out to Jesus with such boldness and persistence, even when faced with opposition or discouragement.

It reminds us that Jesus hears the cries of those who seek Him with a sincere heart, and that He responds with compassion and power.

Moreover, this story is a powerful reminder of the accessibility of Jesus. Despite the throngs of people and the pressing urgency of His journey, Jesus stopped for a blind beggar on the roadside. He didn't just hear Bartimaeus' shout; He responded to it, calling him forward and asking, "What wilt thou that I should do unto thee?" This question, and the subsequent healing, reveals Jesus' deep care for individual needs and His willingness to intervene in the lives of those who seek Him earnestly.

In this book, we will explore the layers of meaning in Bartimaeus' encounter with Jesus, unpacking the significance of his faith, the obstacles he overcame, and the transformation that followed. "The Shout That Stopped The Saviour" is more than a retelling of a miracle; it is an invitation to experience the same transformative power of faith in our own lives, to cry out to Jesus with confidence, and to trust that He hears us, sees us, and stands ready to respond with grace and mercy.

Chapter 1 – Resilience

One of the best examples of resilience in the Bible is the story of Bartimaeus, a blind man who lived in Jericho. His story is found in Mark 10:46-52, and it teaches us a lot about what it means to be resilient in our faith. When Jesus was passing through Jericho, Bartimaeus heard that Jesus was nearby. Even though he was blind and couldn't see Jesus, Bartimaeus began to shout, "Jesus, Son of David, have mercy on me!" The people around him told him to be quiet. They rebuked him and tried to silence him. But Bartimaeus didn't let them stop him. Instead, he shouted even louder, "Son of David, have mercy on me!" This is a powerful example of resilience because Bartimaeus didn't give up, even when others were trying to discourage him. He kept calling out to Jesus because he believed that Jesus could help him. This teaches us that in our own lives, we need to be resilient in our prayers and in seeking God. There will be times when we face discouragement or opposition, but we should keep going and not give up.

Being resilient means having the strength to keep moving forward, even when things are difficult. Bartimaeus showed great strength by continuing to shout for Jesus, despite the crowd telling him to be quiet. This kind of strength is important in our own lives because there will always be challenges and obstacles that try to hold us back. Whether it's people who don't understand our faith or difficult situations that make us feel like giving up, resilience helps us to keep going. For example, imagine you are trying to pray more regularly or read your Bible every day. At first, it might be easy, but then you might get busy with school, friends, or other activities. You might feel tired or distracted and think about skipping your prayer time. This is where resilience comes in. Like Bartimaeus, you need to keep going, even when it's hard. You can set a specific time each day to pray and read your Bible, and make it a priority, just like Bartimaeus made calling out to Jesus a priority.

Another important aspect of resilience is not being afraid to ask for help. Bartimaeus wasn't afraid to shout out to Jesus and ask for mercy. He knew he needed help and wasn't afraid to admit it. Sometimes, being resilient means recognizing that we can't do everything on our own and that we need God's help. It's important to pray and ask God for strength and guidance, just like Bartimaeus asked Jesus for mercy. When we pray, we can ask God to help us be strong and to give us the resilience we need to keep going, even when things are tough. We can also ask others for help and support. Just like Bartimaeus had the crowd around him, we have family, friends, and our church community who can support us and help us stay strong in our faith.

Resilience also means not letting others discourage us. The crowd around Bartimaeus tried to silence him, but he didn't let them stop him. He kept calling out to Jesus because he knew that Jesus could help him. In our own lives, there might be people who don't understand our faith or who try to discourage us. They might say things that make us feel like giving up or that make us doubt ourselves. But like Bartimaeus, we need to stay focused on Jesus and not let others discourage us. We can remember that God loves us and has a plan for our lives, and we can trust Him to help us through difficult times.

One way to build resilience is to focus on positive things and to remind ourselves of God's promises. When we face challenges, it's easy to get discouraged and to focus on the negative. But if we focus on positive things and remind ourselves of God's promises, it can help us stay strong. For example, we can remember that God promises to be with us and to help us. In Isaiah 41:10, it says, "Fear thou not; for I am with thee: be not dismayed; for I am thy God: I will strengthen thee; yea, I will help thee; yea, I will uphold thee with the right hand of my righteousness." This promise reminds us that God is with us and will help us, no matter what we face. By focusing on positive things and reminding ourselves of God's promises, we can build resilience and stay strong in our faith.

Another way to build resilience is to take care of ourselves physically, emotionally, and spiritually. Bartimaeus showed resilience by continuing to shout for Jesus, but he also took action by getting up and going to Jesus when He called him. This shows us that resilience involves both mental strength and taking action. Taking care of ourselves physically can help us have the energy and strength we need to face challenges. This means eating healthy foods, getting enough sleep, and staying active. Taking care of ourselves emotionally means finding ways to cope with stress and difficult emotions. This might include talking to a trusted friend or family member, writing in a journal, or finding activities that help us relax and feel happy. Taking care of ourselves spiritually means spending time with God through prayer, reading the Bible, and attending church. When we take care of ourselves in these ways, it can help us build resilience and stay strong in our faith.

Resilience also means having hope and staying positive, even when things are tough. Bartimaeus had hope that Jesus could heal him, and this hope kept him going, even when the crowd tried to silence him. Having hope means believing that things can get better and that God has a good plan for our lives. It means trusting that God can bring good out of even the most difficult situations. When we have hope, it helps us stay positive and keep going, even when things are tough. We can pray and ask God to help us have hope and to show us the good things He has in store for us. We can also encourage others and help them have hope, just like Bartimaeus' story encourages us.

Resilience is also about learning from our experiences and using them to grow stronger. Bartimaeus' experience of being blind and then being healed by Jesus was a powerful testimony that he could share with others. In our own lives, we can learn from our experiences, both good and bad, and use them to grow stronger in our faith. We can think about times when we faced challenges and how God helped us through them. These experiences can remind us that God is always with us and that we can trust Him to help us. By learning from our experiences and using them to grow stronger, we can build resilience and stay strong in our faith.

Another important part of resilience is perseverance, which means keeping going, even when it's hard. Bartimaeus persevered in calling out to Jesus, even when the crowd told him to be quiet. He didn't give up because he believed that Jesus could help him. In our own lives, we need to persevere in our faith, even when it's hard. This means continuing to pray, read the Bible, and seek God, even when we feel like giving up. It means trusting that God is with us and that He will help us, no matter what we face. By persevering in our faith, we can build resilience and stay strong.

Resilience also involves having a positive mindset and believing that we can overcome challenges. Bartimaeus believed that Jesus could heal him, and this belief gave him the strength to keep going. In our own lives, having a positive mindset can help us stay strong in the face of challenges. We can remind ourselves that with God's help, we can overcome anything. We can pray and ask God to help us stay positive and to give us the strength we need to face challenges. By having a positive mindset and believing that we can overcome challenges, we can build resilience and stay strong in our faith.

In addition to having a positive mindset, resilience involves being adaptable and flexible. Bartimaeus was adaptable in his situation. Even though he was blind, he found a way to get Jesus' attention by shouting out. He didn't let his blindness stop him from seeking Jesus. In our own lives, being adaptable and flexible can help us build resilience. This means being open to change and finding new ways to overcome challenges. It means being willing to try new things and to adjust our plans when things don't go as expected. By being adaptable and flexible, we can build resilience and stay strong in our faith.

Another important aspect of resilience is having a support system. Bartimaeus had people around him, and although they tried to silence him, he still had the crowd around him. In our own lives, having a support system can help us build resilience. This means having family, friends, and a church community who can support us and help us stay strong in our faith. We can talk to our support system when we're facing challenges and ask for their prayers and encouragement. By having a support system, we can build resilience and stay strong in our faith.

Resilience also involves being proactive and taking action. Bartimaeus didn't just sit and wait for Jesus to come to him; he took action by shouting out and then getting up to go to Jesus when He called him. In our own lives, being proactive and taking action can help us build resilience. This means taking steps to overcome challenges and to seek God's help. It means not just waiting for things to get better but taking action to make them better. By being proactive and taking action, we can build resilience and stay strong in our faith.

In conclusion, resilience is a key part of our faith and relationship with God. Bartimaeus' story teaches us the importance of being resilient in our prayers and in seeking God. It shows us that

we need to have strength, hope, and a positive mindset, and to be adaptable and flexible. It also teaches us the importance of having a support system, being proactive, and taking care of ourselves physically, emotionally, and spiritually. By building resilience, we can stay strong in our faith and overcome any challenges we face. We can trust that God is with us and that He will help us, no matter what we face. Just like Bartimaeus, we can call out to Jesus and trust that He hears us and will help us. By being resilient, we can stay strong in our faith and grow closer to God.

Chapter 2 – Recognition

Bartimaeus was a blind beggar who lived in Jericho. When he heard that Jesus of Nazareth was passing by, he began to shout, "Jesus, Son of David, have mercy on me!" This phrase, "Son of David," was significant because it recognized Jesus as the Messiah, the promised Savior of the Jewish people who would come from the lineage of King David. Even though Bartimaeus was physically blind, he saw something that many others did not—he saw Jesus for who He truly was. This recognition is powerful because it shows that spiritual insight is more important than physical sight. Bartimaeus, despite his blindness, had the faith to see Jesus as the Messiah. This recognition of Christ is something that every Christian should strive for in their daily lives. Recognizing Jesus' true identity means understanding and acknowledging Him as the Messiah and Savior, not just in words, but in how we live our lives.

Recognizing Christ involves a deep understanding of who He is and what He has done for us. Jesus is not just a historical figure or a great teacher; He is the Son of God who came to save us from our sins. This understanding should influence every aspect of our lives. When we recognize Jesus as the Messiah, we see Him as the fulfillment of God's promises in the Old Testament. The title "Son of David" connects Jesus to the prophecies about the Messiah who would come to establish God's kingdom. This recognition calls for us to honor Jesus in our thoughts, words, and actions. It means putting Him first in our lives and allowing His teachings to guide our decisions.

Bartimaeus' recognition of Jesus as the "Son of David" also shows the importance of faith. Despite his blindness, Bartimaeus believed in Jesus' power to heal him. His faith was so strong that he was willing to shout out and persist even when the crowd tried to silence him. This teaches us that recognizing Christ involves having faith in Him, even when it is difficult. Faith is the foundation of our relationship with Jesus. It means trusting Him and believing in His power to transform our lives. Like Bartimaeus, we need to have a strong faith that persists despite challenges and opposition. Our recognition of Christ should be evident in our unwavering faith and trust in Him.

Furthermore, recognizing Christ means acknowledging His authority and lordship over our lives. Jesus is not just our Savior but also our Lord. This means that He has the authority to guide and direct our lives. When we recognize Christ as our Lord, we submit to His will and follow His commandments. This submission is a sign of our trust and faith in Him. It means that we are willing to let go of our own plans and desires and seek to do His will. This is a daily commitment that requires humility and obedience. By recognizing Jesus' authority, we show our devotion and commitment to Him.

In addition to recognizing Jesus' authority, honoring His true identity involves worship. Worship is an expression of our love and reverence for Jesus. It is a way for us to acknowledge His greatness and thank Him for His sacrifice. Worship can take many forms, including prayer, singing, reading the Bible, and serving others. By making worship a regular part of our lives, we show that we recognize and honor Jesus as our Messiah and Savior. Worship is not just an activity but a lifestyle that reflects our recognition of Christ. It is a way for us to stay connected to Him and grow in our relationship with Him.

Another important aspect of recognizing Christ is acknowledging His role as our Redeemer. Jesus came to earth to save us from our sins and to offer us eternal life. This act of redemption is the greatest demonstration of God's love for us. When we recognize Jesus as our Redeemer, we understand the magnitude of His sacrifice and the depth of His love. This recognition should fill us with gratitude and inspire us to live our lives in a way that honors Him. It means accepting His gift of salvation and living a life that reflects His love and grace. Recognizing Jesus as our Redeemer also means sharing the good news of His salvation with others. It is our responsibility to spread the message of Jesus' love and sacrifice to those around us.

Bartimaeus' recognition of Jesus also highlights the importance of seeking Him earnestly. Bartimaeus did not hesitate to call out to Jesus when he heard that He was passing by. He recognized the opportunity to encounter the Messiah and seized it with urgency. This teaches us that recognizing Christ involves actively seeking Him in our daily lives. We should not wait for the perfect moment to seek Jesus; instead, we should seek Him earnestly and passionately every day. This means making time for prayer, reading the Bible, and spending time in His presence. By seeking Jesus earnestly, we show that we recognize His importance in our lives and desire a deeper relationship with Him.

Additionally, recognizing Christ means being transformed by His presence. When Bartimaeus encountered Jesus, his life was changed forever. He received his sight and became a follower of Jesus. This transformation is a testament to the power of recognizing Christ. When we truly recognize Jesus as our Messiah and Savior, our lives should be transformed. This transformation is not just a one-time event but a continuous process of becoming more like Jesus. It means allowing Him to change our hearts, minds, and actions. By being transformed by Jesus, we reflect His love and grace to the world.

Recognizing Christ also involves living a life of service. Jesus came to serve and to give His life as a ransom for many. As His followers, we are called to serve others in His name. This means putting the needs of others before our own and showing kindness and compassion to those around us. By serving others, we demonstrate that we recognize and honor Jesus as our Messiah and Savior. Service is a way for us to live out our faith and to show the world the love of Christ. It is a practical way to reflect our recognition of Christ and to make a positive impact on the lives of others.

Furthermore, recognizing Christ means living with hope. Jesus' resurrection from the dead gives us hope for eternal life. This hope should be evident in the way we live our lives. It means having a positive outlook and trusting in God's promises. When we face challenges and difficulties, we can hold on to the hope that Jesus gives us. This hope gives us the strength to persevere and to keep our faith strong. By living with hope, we show that we recognize Jesus' victory over sin and death and that we trust in His promise of eternal life.

In addition to living with hope, recognizing Christ means being a witness for Him. Bartimaeus' recognition of Jesus led to a powerful testimony of faith. He was not afraid to shout out and declare his belief in Jesus. This teaches us that recognizing Christ involves sharing our faith with others. We should not be afraid to talk about Jesus and to share the good news of His salvation. Our lives should be a testimony of His love and grace. By being a witness for Jesus, we help others to recognize Him and to come to faith in Him.

Recognizing Christ also means living a life of integrity. Jesus lived a perfect, sinless life, and we are called to follow His example. This means being honest, trustworthy, and living according to God's commandments. When we live with integrity, we show that we recognize Jesus as our Messiah and Savior. Integrity is a reflection of our faith and a way to honor Jesus in our daily lives. It means doing what is right, even when it is difficult, and being a positive example to others. By living with integrity, we demonstrate our recognition of Christ and our commitment to following Him.

Another important aspect of recognizing Christ is having a heart of gratitude. Bartimaeus' healing was a cause for great gratitude and joy. When we recognize Jesus as our Messiah and Savior, our hearts should be filled with gratitude for all that He has done for us. Gratitude is an important part of our faith because it helps us to focus on God's blessings and to appreciate His love and grace. We can express our gratitude through prayer, worship, and by living a life that honors God. By having a heart of gratitude, we show that we recognize and appreciate Jesus' sacrifice and love.

Recognizing Christ also means being committed to spiritual growth. Bartimaeus' recognition of Jesus led to a deeper relationship with Him. In our own lives, recognizing Jesus as our Messiah and Savior should lead to a commitment to grow spiritually. This means continually seeking to know Jesus more and to become more like Him. We can do this through prayer, reading the Bible, attending church, and being part of a community of believers. Spiritual growth is a lifelong journey, and by committing to it, we show our recognition of Christ and our desire to deepen our relationship with Him.

Furthermore, recognizing Christ involves living a life of compassion. Jesus was known for His compassion and care for others. As His followers, we are called to show compassion to those around us. This means being kind, understanding, and supportive to those in need. By showing compassion, we reflect Jesus' love and demonstrate our recognition of Him as our Messiah and Savior. Compassion is an important part of our faith and a way to make a positive impact on the lives of others. By living a life of compassion, we honor Jesus and show the world what it means to follow Him.

In conclusion, recognizing Christ is a fundamental aspect of our faith and relationship with God. Bartimaeus' story teaches us the importance of recognizing Jesus' true identity as the "Son of David" and the Messiah. This recognition involves understanding and acknowledging Jesus as our Savior, having faith in Him, submitting to His authority, and worshiping Him. It also means living a life that reflects His love and grace, being transformed by His presence, serving others, living with hope, being a witness for Him, living with integrity, having a heart of gratitude, committing to spiritual growth, and showing compassion. By recognizing and honoring Jesus as our Messiah and Savior, we can grow in our faith and relationship with God and make a positive impact on the lives of others.

Chapter 3 – Readiness

When Bartimaeus heard that Jesus of Nazareth was passing by, he didn't hesitate or second-guess himself. Despite being blind and surrounded by a crowd that tried to silence him, Bartimaeus called out loudly, "Jesus, Son of David, have mercy on me!" This readiness to call out to Jesus shows his faith and his belief that Jesus could and would help him. Bartimaeus' readiness to act, even in the face of obstacles, is a lesson for all of us. It teaches us that when we have faith, we need to be ready to act on it. Faith is not just about believing in our hearts; it's about being willing to take action, to step out in confidence, and to trust that Jesus hears us and responds to us.

In our own lives, readiness to act means being prepared to take steps in faith, even when we face challenges or discouragement. It means not waiting for the perfect moment but being willing to seize the opportunities that God gives us. Like Bartimaeus, we need to recognize when Jesus is passing by and be ready to call out to Him. This readiness is a sign of our faith and trust in Jesus. It shows that we believe in His power to help us and that we are willing to take action to seek His help. Being ready to call out to Jesus means that we are always prepared to turn to Him in prayer, no matter what situation we find ourselves in. It means that we have a mindset of faith, always looking to Jesus and being ready to rely on Him.

Readiness also involves having a sense of urgency in our faith. Bartimaeus didn't wait for another opportunity; he acted immediately when he heard that Jesus was near. This sense of urgency is important because it shows that we value our relationship with Jesus and understand the importance of seeking Him. When we are ready to act in faith, we don't put off our prayers or our actions. We don't wait for everything to be perfect. Instead, we move forward, trusting that Jesus will meet us where we are. This urgency in our faith is a sign that we are serious about our relationship with Jesus and that we recognize the importance of seeking Him first.

Another important aspect of readiness is persistence. Bartimaeus continued to call out to Jesus, even when the crowd tried to silence him. This persistence shows that he was not easily discouraged and that he was determined to reach Jesus. In our own lives, being ready to act in faith means being persistent, even when we face obstacles. It means not giving up when things get tough but continuing to seek Jesus with all our hearts. This persistence is a sign of our trust in Jesus and our belief that He will respond to us. When we are persistent in our faith, we show that we are committed to our relationship with Jesus and that we trust Him to help us, no matter what we face.

Readiness to act in faith also means being willing to take risks. Bartimaeus took a risk by calling out to Jesus in front of the crowd. He didn't know how Jesus would respond, but he was willing to take that chance because he believed in Jesus' power to heal him. In our own lives, being ready to act in faith means being willing to step out of our comfort zones and take risks for Jesus. It means being willing to do things that might be difficult or uncomfortable because we trust that Jesus will be with us and help us. This willingness to take risks is a sign of our faith and our trust in Jesus. It shows that we are not afraid to step out in faith because we know that Jesus is with us.

In addition to being willing to take risks, readiness to act in faith means being open to God's timing. Bartimaeus didn't wait for a more convenient time to call out to Jesus; he acted immediately when he heard that Jesus was near. This openness to God's timing is important because it shows that we trust God's plan for our lives. It means that we are willing to act when God calls us, even if the timing doesn't seem perfect to us. When we are ready to act in faith, we show that we trust God's timing and that we are willing to follow His lead. This openness to God's timing is a sign of our faith and our trust in God's plan for our lives.

Readiness to act in faith also involves being willing to seek help. Bartimaeus wasn't afraid to call out to Jesus and ask for help. He recognized that he needed Jesus' help and wasn't afraid to admit it. In our own lives, being ready to act in faith means being willing to seek help from Jesus and from others. It means recognizing that we can't do everything on our own and that we need God's help. This willingness to seek help is a sign of our humility and our trust in Jesus. It shows that we recognize our own limitations and that we are willing to rely on Jesus for strength and guidance.

Another important aspect of readiness is having a positive attitude. Bartimaeus had a positive attitude because he believed that Jesus could help him. He didn't let his blindness or the crowd's discouragement stop him from seeking Jesus. In our own lives, being ready to act in faith means having a positive attitude and believing that Jesus can and will help us. It means not letting negative thoughts or doubts hold us back. This positive attitude is a sign of our faith and our trust in Jesus. It shows that we believe in Jesus' power to help us and that we are willing to take action to seek His help.

Readiness to act in faith also involves being prepared. Bartimaeus was prepared to call out to Jesus when he heard that He was near. He didn't hesitate or second-guess himself; he acted immediately. In our own lives, being ready to act in faith means being prepared to seek Jesus at any moment. It means being in a constant state of readiness, always looking to Jesus and being prepared to turn to Him in prayer. This readiness is a sign of our faith and our trust in Jesus. It shows that we are always prepared to seek Jesus and to rely on Him.

In addition to being prepared, readiness to act in faith means being willing to take the first step. Bartimaeus took the first step by calling out to Jesus. He didn't wait for Jesus to come to him; he took the initiative to seek Jesus. In our own lives, being ready to act in faith means being willing to take the first step, even if it's difficult. It means being proactive in our faith and taking the initiative to seek Jesus. This willingness to take the first step is a sign of our faith and our trust in Jesus. It shows that we are willing to take action to seek Jesus and to rely on Him.

Another important aspect of readiness is being willing to be vulnerable. Bartimaeus was willing to be vulnerable by calling out to Jesus in front of the crowd. He didn't let his fear of being judged or rejected stop him from seeking Jesus. In our own lives, being ready to act in faith means being willing to be vulnerable and to seek Jesus with all our hearts. It means being honest about our needs and our struggles and being willing to ask for help. This willingness to be vulnerable is a sign of our faith and our trust in Jesus. It shows that we are willing to seek Jesus with all our hearts and to rely on Him for help.

Readiness to act in faith also involves being willing to persevere. Bartimaeus didn't give up when the crowd tried to silence him; he continued to call out to Jesus. This perseverance shows that he was determined to reach Jesus. In our own lives, being ready to act in faith means being willing to persevere, even when we face obstacles. It means not giving up when things get tough but continuing to seek Jesus with all our hearts. This perseverance is a sign of our faith and our trust in Jesus. It shows that we are committed to our relationship with Jesus and that we trust Him to help us, no matter what we face.

In addition to perseverance, readiness to act in faith means being willing to take responsibility for our actions. Bartimaeus took responsibility for his actions by calling out to Jesus and seeking His help. He didn't wait for someone else to help him; he took the initiative to seek Jesus. In our own lives, being ready to act in faith means being willing to take responsibility for our actions and to seek Jesus with all our hearts. It means not waiting for someone else to take the first step but being proactive in our faith. This willingness to take responsibility is a sign of our faith and our trust in Jesus. It shows that we are willing to take action to seek Jesus and to rely on Him.

Readiness to act in faith also involves being willing to be open to God's will. Bartimaeus was open to God's will by seeking Jesus and asking for His help. He recognized that he needed Jesus' help and was willing to accept whatever Jesus had for him. In our own lives, being ready to act in faith means being willing to be open to God's will and to seek Jesus with all our hearts. It means being willing to accept whatever God has for us and to trust that His plan is best. This willingness to be open to God's will is a sign of our faith and our trust in Jesus. It shows that we are willing to seek Jesus with all our hearts and to rely on Him for guidance and direction.

In conclusion, Bartimaeus' readiness to call out to Jesus is a powerful example of faith in action. His story teaches us the importance of being ready to act in faith, even in the face of obstacles. It shows us that readiness involves being prepared, having a sense of urgency, being persistent, taking risks, being open to God's timing, seeking help, having a positive attitude, being proactive, taking the first step, being vulnerable, persevering, taking responsibility, and being open to God's will. By being ready to act in faith, we show our trust in Jesus and our belief in His power to help us. This readiness is a sign of our faith and our commitment to our relationship with Jesus. It shows that we are always prepared to seek Jesus and to rely on Him for help and guidance. Just like Bartimaeus, we can be ready to call out to Jesus and trust that He hears us and will respond to us. By being ready to act in faith, we can grow in our relationship with Jesus and experience the power of His love and grace in our lives.

Chapter 4 – Resolve

When Bartimaeus heard that Jesus of Nazareth was passing by, he began to shout, "Jesus, Son of David, have mercy on me!" The crowd around him tried to silence him, telling him to be quiet and stop bothering Jesus. But Bartimaeus did not let their attempts to silence him deter his efforts. Instead, he shouted even louder, "Son of David, have mercy on me!" This unwavering resolve to reach Jesus despite the crowd's discouragement shows a powerful lesson for all of us. It teaches us that in our own lives, we need to have the resolve to overcome obstacles and distractions that try to keep us from growing closer to God and fulfilling His purpose for our lives. Bartimaeus' determination to reach Jesus is a testament to his faith and his belief that Jesus could heal him. This kind of resolve is essential for our spiritual growth and relationship with God. It means not giving up when we face difficulties but pressing on with determination and trust in God's plan for us.

In our daily lives, we often encounter obstacles and distractions that can hinder our spiritual growth. These can come in many forms, such as negative influences, doubts, fears, and even our busy schedules. Just like Bartimaeus, we need to have the resolve to push through these obstacles and stay focused on our goal of growing closer to God. This means making time for prayer, reading the Bible, attending church, and seeking fellowship with other believers. It also means staying committed to our faith even when it is not easy. Bartimaeus did not let the crowd's attempts to silence him stop him from seeking Jesus, and we should not let anything stop us from seeking a deeper relationship with God.

One of the key aspects of resolve is persistence. Bartimaeus was persistent in his efforts to reach Jesus. He did not give up when the crowd told him to be quiet. Instead, he shouted even louder, determined to get Jesus' attention. This persistence is a crucial part of resolve because it shows that we are committed to our goal and are willing to keep trying, no matter how many obstacles we face. In our spiritual lives, persistence means continuing to seek God and follow His will, even when it is difficult. It means praying consistently, even when we do not see immediate answers, and trusting that God is working in our lives, even when we do not understand His plan. By being persistent in our faith, we show our resolve to grow closer to God and to fulfill His purpose for our lives.

Another important aspect of resolve is courage. Bartimaeus showed great courage by calling out to Jesus in front of the crowd. He was not afraid to make his needs known, even though the crowd tried to silence him. This courage is essential for us as well. We need to have the courage to stand up for our faith and to seek God, even when it is not popular or when others try to discourage us. This means being bold in our prayers, sharing our faith with others, and living according to God's principles, even when it is challenging. By having the courage to seek God and to follow His will, we demonstrate our resolve and our commitment to our relationship with Him.

In addition to persistence and courage, resolve also involves having a clear focus. Bartimaeus was focused on reaching Jesus. He did not let the crowd's attempts to silence him distract him from his goal. This clear focus is important for us as well. We need to keep our eyes on Jesus and not let the distractions of life pull us away from our relationship with Him. This means setting priorities and making time for the things that help us grow spiritually. It also means being aware of the things that can distract us from our faith and making a conscious effort to avoid them. By keeping a clear focus on Jesus, we can stay resolved to grow closer to Him and to fulfill His purpose for our lives.

Another key aspect of resolve is determination. Bartimaeus was determined to reach Jesus, no matter what. He did not let the crowd's discouragement stop him. This determination is vital for our spiritual growth as well. We need to be determined to follow God's will and to seek Him with all our hearts. This means not giving up when we face challenges and being willing to do whatever it takes to grow in our faith. By being determined in our relationship with God, we show our resolve and our commitment to Him.

Resolve also involves having faith. Bartimaeus had faith that Jesus could heal him, and this faith gave him the strength to keep calling out, even when the crowd tried to silence him. Faith is a crucial part of resolve because it gives us the confidence to keep going, even when we face obstacles. It means trusting that God is with us and that He will help us overcome the challenges we face. By having faith in God's promises and His love for us, we can stay resolved to grow closer to Him and to fulfill His purpose for our lives.

In addition to faith, resolve also means having hope. Bartimaeus had hope that Jesus would hear him and have mercy on him. This hope kept him going, even when the crowd tried to discourage him. Hope is important for us as well because it gives us the motivation to keep seeking God, even when things are difficult. It means believing that God has a good plan for our lives and that He will help us overcome the obstacles we face. By having hope in God's promises, we can stay resolved to grow closer to Him and to fulfill His purpose for our lives.

Another important aspect of resolve is patience. Bartimaeus showed patience by continuing to call out to Jesus, even when he did not get an immediate response. This patience is essential for our spiritual growth as well. We need to be patient in our relationship with God, trusting that He will answer our prayers in His perfect timing. This means not getting discouraged when we do not see immediate results and continuing to seek God with a patient heart. By being patient in our faith, we show our resolve to grow closer to God and to fulfill His purpose for our lives.

Resolve also involves perseverance. Bartimaeus persevered in his efforts to reach Jesus, despite the crowd's attempts to silence him. Perseverance is crucial for our spiritual growth because it means continuing to seek God and follow His will, even when we face challenges. It means not giving up when things get tough and trusting that God is with us, helping us to overcome the obstacles we face. By persevering in our faith, we show our resolve to grow closer to God and to fulfill His purpose for our lives.

In addition to perseverance, resolve also means being steadfast. Bartimaeus was steadfast in his determination to reach Jesus. He did not waver in his efforts, despite the crowd's attempts to silence him. This steadfastness is important for us as well. We need to be steadfast in our faith, standing firm in our commitment to God, no matter what challenges we face. This means being consistent in our prayers, our worship, and our obedience to God's will. By being steadfast in our faith, we show our resolve to grow closer to God and to fulfill His purpose for our lives.

Another key aspect of resolve is resilience. Bartimaeus showed resilience by continuing to call out to Jesus, even when the crowd tried to silence him. This resilience is important for us as well because it means bouncing back from setbacks and continuing to seek God, no matter what obstacles we face. It means not letting difficulties discourage us and trusting that God is with us, helping us to overcome the challenges we face. By being resilient in our faith, we show our resolve to grow closer to God and to fulfill His purpose for our lives.

Resolve also involves being proactive. Bartimaeus was proactive in his efforts to reach Jesus. He did not wait for Jesus to come to him; he took the initiative to call out to Jesus and seek His help. This proactive attitude is important for us as well because it means taking action to grow in our faith and to seek God. It means not waiting for things to happen but being intentional in our efforts to grow closer to God. By being proactive in our faith, we show our resolve to grow closer to God and to fulfill His purpose for our lives.

In addition to being proactive, resolve also means being committed. Bartimaeus was committed to reaching Jesus, no matter what. This commitment is essential for our spiritual growth as well.

We need to be committed to our relationship with God, making it a priority in our lives. This means being dedicated to our prayers, our worship, and our obedience to God's will. By being committed in our faith, we show our resolve to grow closer to God and to fulfill His purpose for our lives.

Resolve also involves having a positive attitude. Bartimaeus had a positive attitude because he believed that Jesus could heal him. This positive attitude is important for us as well because it means having faith and hope in God's promises. It means believing that God can and will help us overcome the challenges we face. By having a positive attitude in our faith, we show our resolve to grow closer to God and to fulfill His purpose for our lives.

Another important aspect of resolve is having a clear vision. Bartimaeus had a clear vision of what he wanted: to be healed by Jesus. This clear vision is important for us as well because it means knowing what we want to achieve in our relationship with God. It means having a clear goal of growing closer to God and fulfilling His purpose for our lives. By having a clear vision in our faith, we show our resolve to grow closer to God and to fulfill His purpose for our lives.

In addition to having a clear vision, resolve also means being flexible. Bartimaeus was flexible in his efforts to reach Jesus. He did not let the crowd's attempts to silence him stop him from seeking Jesus. This flexibility is important for us as well because it means being adaptable in our relationship with God. It means being willing to change our plans and to trust that God's plan is best. By being flexible in our faith, we show our resolve to grow closer to God and to fulfill His purpose for our lives.

Resolve also involves being disciplined. Bartimaeus showed discipline by continuing to call out to Jesus, despite the crowd's attempts to silence him. This discipline is important for us as well because it means being consistent in our efforts to grow in our faith. It means making time for prayer, reading the Bible, and seeking fellowship with other believers. By being disciplined in our faith, we show our resolve to grow closer to God and to fulfill His purpose for our lives.

In addition to being disciplined, resolve also means being resourceful. Bartimaeus was resourceful in his efforts to reach Jesus. He did not let his blindness stop him from seeking Jesus. This resourcefulness is important for us as well because it means finding ways to grow in our faith, no matter what obstacles we face. It means being creative and using the resources available to us to seek God and to grow closer to Him. By being resourceful in our faith, we show our resolve to grow closer to God and to fulfill His purpose for our lives.

Another key aspect of resolve is having a support system. Bartimaeus had people around him, and despite their attempts to silence him, he continued to call out to Jesus. This support system is important for us as well because it means having family, friends, and a church community who can support us in our faith. It means seeking fellowship with other believers and being part of a community that encourages us to grow in our relationship with God. By having a support system in our faith, we show our resolve to grow closer to God and to fulfill His purpose for our lives.

In conclusion, Bartimaeus' resolve to reach Jesus is a powerful example of faith in action. His story teaches us the importance of having the resolve to overcome obstacles and distractions that try to keep us from growing closer to God and fulfilling His purpose for our lives. It shows us that resolve involves persistence, courage, a clear focus, determination, faith, hope, patience, perseverance, steadfastness, resilience, being proactive, committed, having a positive attitude, a clear vision, flexibility, discipline, resourcefulness, and having a support system. By having the resolve to grow closer to God and to seek His will for our lives, we can overcome the challenges we face and experience the fullness of God's love and purpose for us. Just like Bartimaeus, we can have the resolve to call out to Jesus and trust that He hears us and will respond to us. By being resolved in our faith, we can grow in our relationship with God and fulfill His purpose for our lives.

Chapter 5 – Receptiveness

When Bartimaeus heard that Jesus was passing by, he began to shout, "Jesus, Son of David, have mercy on me!" Despite the crowd's attempts to silence him, Bartimaeus continued to cry out, demonstrating his faith and desperation. Jesus, hearing Bartimaeus' cries, stopped and commanded him to be called. This moment is crucial because it shows Jesus' willingness to stop and listen to someone in need, no matter how insignificant they might seem to others. Jesus' receptiveness to Bartimaeus teaches us about His character and how He interacts with us. Jesus didn't ignore Bartimaeus or pass him by; He responded with compassion and attention. This act of stopping and calling Bartimaeus is a powerful demonstration of Jesus' love and receptiveness. It shows that Jesus is always willing to listen and respond to our needs, no matter how small or big they might be.

The story of Bartimaeus reassures us that Jesus is attentive to our cries for help. Just as He was receptive to Bartimaeus, He is receptive to us. This means that when we call out to Jesus in prayer, He hears us and responds. We can trust in Jesus' receptiveness and love, knowing that He is always ready to listen to our needs and provide us with the help we require. This is a comforting and encouraging thought because it means we are never alone in our struggles. Jesus is always there, ready to stop and attend to our needs, just as He did for Bartimaeus.

Jesus' receptiveness also teaches us about the importance of being open and honest in our relationship with Him. Bartimaeus was not afraid to cry out for help, despite the crowd's attempts to silence him. He was open about his need and his faith in Jesus. This openness and honesty are essential in our own relationship with Jesus. We need to be willing to come to Him with our needs, fears, and desires, trusting that He will listen and respond with love and compassion. Jesus' receptiveness encourages us to be vulnerable and honest in our prayers, knowing that He cares deeply about us and is always ready to help.

Furthermore, Jesus' response to Bartimaeus shows us that He values each individual, regardless of their social status or condition. Bartimaeus was a blind beggar, someone who was likely marginalized and overlooked by society. Yet, Jesus stopped for him and called him forward. This act demonstrates that Jesus sees and values every person, no matter their circumstances. It reminds us that we are all important to Jesus, and He is receptive to each one of us. This inclusiveness and love are central to Jesus' character and His message of the Gospel.

Jesus' receptiveness also highlights the importance of faith. Bartimaeus' faith was evident in his persistent cries for Jesus' help. Despite the crowd's discouragement, he believed that Jesus could and would heal him. Jesus recognized this faith and responded to it. This teaches us that our faith is important to Jesus. When we come to Him in faith, believing in His power and love, He responds. Our faith opens the door for Jesus to work in our lives and meet our needs. Just as Bartimaeus' faith led to his healing, our faith can lead to Jesus' intervention in our lives.

In addition, Jesus' receptiveness demonstrates His compassion. By stopping and calling Bartimaeus, Jesus showed His deep compassion for those who are suffering. He didn't just hear Bartimaeus; He felt compassion for him and took action to help him. This compassion is a key aspect of Jesus' character. He cares deeply about our pain and struggles, and He is moved to help us. This compassion reassures us that Jesus understands our suffering and is always ready to offer His love and support.

Jesus' receptiveness also encourages us to be receptive to others. Just as Jesus was open and attentive to Bartimaeus, we are called to be open and attentive to those around us who are in need. This means listening to others, showing compassion, and being willing to help. By being receptive to others, we can reflect Jesus' love and compassion in our own lives. This receptiveness is an important part of our Christian faith and our call to love others as Jesus loves us.

Moreover, Jesus' receptiveness to Bartimaeus reminds us of the importance of taking action. Jesus didn't just listen to Bartimaeus; He took action to help him. This teaches us that our receptiveness should be accompanied by action. When we see someone in need, we should not just listen; we should also take steps to help them. This action-oriented receptiveness is a powerful way to demonstrate our faith and love for others. It shows that we are not just passive listeners but active participants in helping those in need.

Jesus' receptiveness also shows us the power of mercy. When Bartimaeus called out for mercy, Jesus responded. This response highlights the importance of mercy in Jesus' ministry and in our own lives. We are called to show mercy to others, just as Jesus shows mercy to us. This means forgiving others, showing compassion, and being willing to help those who are suffering. By being merciful, we can reflect Jesus' love and compassion in our own lives.

In addition, Jesus' receptiveness teaches us about the importance of hope. Bartimaeus had hope that Jesus would hear him and respond. This hope gave him the courage to keep calling out, despite the crowd's attempts to silence him. This hope is important for us as well. When we face challenges and difficulties, we can have hope that Jesus will hear us and respond. This hope gives us the strength to keep going and to trust in Jesus' love and compassion.

Jesus' receptiveness also encourages us to have patience. Bartimaeus showed patience by continuing to call out to Jesus, even when he did not get an immediate response. This patience is important for us as well. We need to be patient in our relationship with Jesus, trusting that He will respond in His perfect timing. This patience shows our faith and trust in Jesus, knowing that He hears us and will answer our prayers in the best way possible.

Furthermore, Jesus' receptiveness teaches us about the importance of being persistent. Bartimaeus was persistent in his cries for help, and Jesus responded to his persistence. This persistence is important for us as well. We need to be persistent in our prayers and in seeking Jesus, even when we face obstacles or delays. This persistence shows our determination and faith, and it opens the door for Jesus to work in our lives.

Jesus' receptiveness also reminds us of the importance of having a humble heart. Bartimaeus approached Jesus with humility, recognizing his need for mercy. This humility is important for us as well. We need to approach Jesus with a humble heart, recognizing our need for His help and mercy. This humility shows our dependence on Jesus and our trust in His love and compassion.

In addition, Jesus' receptiveness teaches us about the importance of being open to God's will. Bartimaeus was open to whatever Jesus had for him, and this openness allowed Jesus to work in his life. This openness is important for us as well. We need to be open to God's will, trusting that His plan is best for us. This openness shows our faith and trust in God, and it allows Him to work in our lives in powerful ways.

Jesus' receptiveness also encourages us to have a heart of gratitude. Bartimaeus' response to Jesus' call was one of gratitude and joy. This gratitude is important for us as well. When we recognize Jesus' receptiveness and His work in our lives, we should respond with gratitude. This gratitude shows our appreciation for Jesus' love and compassion, and it strengthens our relationship with Him.

Moreover, Jesus' receptiveness teaches us about the importance of faith. Bartimaeus' faith was evident in his persistent cries for Jesus' help. This faith is important for us as well. We need to have faith in Jesus' power and love, trusting that He will respond to our needs. This faith opens the door for Jesus to work in our lives and to meet our needs.

Jesus' receptiveness also reminds us of the importance of being receptive to others. Just as Jesus was open and attentive to Bartimaeus, we are called to be open and attentive to those around us who are in need. This means listening to others, showing compassion, and being willing to help. By being receptive to others, we can reflect Jesus' love and compassion in our own lives.

In conclusion, the story of Bartimaeus in Mark 10:46-52 highlights Jesus' receptiveness to those in need. Jesus stopped and called Bartimaeus, showing His willingness to listen and respond to someone in need. This receptiveness teaches us about Jesus' character and His love for us. It reassures us that Jesus is always willing to listen and respond to our needs, no matter how small or big they might be. It encourages us to be open and honest in our relationship with Jesus, knowing that He cares deeply about us and is always ready to help. It also reminds us of the importance of being receptive to others and taking action to help those in need. By being receptive to Jesus and to others, we can grow in our relationship with Him and reflect His love and compassion in our own lives. This receptiveness is a powerful demonstration of our faith and our commitment to following Jesus' example. It shows that we are not just passive listeners but active participants in helping those in need and growing closer to God. By trusting in Jesus' receptiveness and love, we can experience the fullness of His compassion and grace in our lives, just as Bartimaeus did.

Chapter 6 – Response

When Bartimaeus heard that Jesus was passing by, he didn't hesitate to shout out, "Jesus, Son of David, have mercy on me!" Even when the crowd tried to silence him, Bartimaeus persisted, showing his determination and faith. His persistence paid off because Jesus stopped and called him. At that moment, Bartimaeus didn't delay; he threw aside his cloak, jumped to his feet, and went to Jesus. This immediate response is significant because it shows Bartimaeus' eagerness and urgency to come to Jesus without letting anything hold him back. By casting aside his cloak, which was likely his only possession and source of warmth and security, Bartimaeus demonstrated his willingness to leave behind anything that could hinder his approach to Jesus. This act of casting aside his garment and rising to come to Jesus symbolizes leaving behind his past life and fully embracing the new life that Jesus offered.

This immediate and wholehearted response to Jesus' call is an important lesson for us. When Jesus calls us, whether it's through a prompting in our hearts, through scripture, or through life circumstances, we should respond promptly and without hesitation. Delaying our response can lead to missed opportunities and blessings. Just as Bartimaeus seized the moment to meet Jesus, we should be ready to act when we sense Jesus calling us. This kind of prompt response requires us to be attentive and sensitive to Jesus' voice. It means being in a constant state of readiness, always looking for and listening to God's guidance in our lives.

Moreover, Bartimaeus' action of casting aside his cloak teaches us about the importance of letting go of anything that hinders our approach to Jesus. In our own lives, there are many things that can hold us back from fully responding to Jesus' call. These could be physical possessions, unhealthy relationships, habits, fears, or doubts. Bartimaeus' willingness to leave his cloak behind encourages us to identify and let go of whatever might be hindering us from fully coming to Jesus. It means being willing to make sacrifices and changes in our lives to follow Him more closely. This could involve letting go of material possessions that we hold too dearly, breaking free from negative influences, or overcoming personal fears and insecurities that prevent us from stepping out in faith.

Another aspect of Bartimaeus' response is his faith and trust in Jesus. By immediately going to Jesus, Bartimaeus demonstrated his belief that Jesus could and would help him. This kind of faith is essential for us as well. When we respond to Jesus' call, we need to do so with faith and trust in His power and goodness. It means believing that Jesus has our best interests at heart and that He will provide for us and guide us. This faith gives us the confidence to leave behind our old ways and embrace the new life that Jesus offers.

Additionally, Bartimaeus' response shows his humility and recognition of his need for Jesus. By calling out to Jesus and then immediately going to Him when called, Bartimaeus acknowledged that he needed Jesus' help and was willing to seek it. In our own lives, responding to Jesus' call involves recognizing our own need for Him and being willing to seek His help and guidance. It means admitting that we cannot do it on our own and that we need Jesus' strength and wisdom in our lives. This humility and dependence on Jesus are crucial for our spiritual growth and relationship with Him.

Bartimaeus' response also highlights the importance of taking action. It wasn't enough for him to just call out to Jesus; he had to take the step of going to Jesus when called. In the same way, our response to Jesus' call should involve action. It means not just acknowledging Jesus' call in our hearts but also taking concrete steps to follow Him. This could involve changes in our behavior, making new commitments, or taking on new responsibilities in our faith journey. By taking action, we demonstrate our commitment to Jesus and our willingness to follow Him wherever He leads.

Furthermore, Bartimaeus' response shows his readiness to embrace the new life that Jesus offered. By casting aside his cloak and going to Jesus, he symbolized his readiness to leave his old life behind and embrace a new beginning. This readiness is important for us as well. Responding to Jesus' call means being willing to leave behind our past mistakes, failures, and old ways of living, and embracing the new life that Jesus offers. It means being open to transformation and renewal in our lives. Jesus calls us to a life of abundance and purpose, and responding to His call involves being willing to step into this new life with faith and trust.

Bartimaeus' story also teaches us about the joy and fulfillment that come from responding to Jesus' call. When Bartimaeus came to Jesus, he received his sight and was able to follow Jesus along the road. This transformation brought him not only physical healing but also spiritual renewal and a new sense of purpose. In the same way, when we respond to Jesus' call, we can experience the joy and fulfillment that come from living in alignment with God's will. It brings us closer to Jesus and allows us to experience His love, grace, and blessings in our lives.

Moreover, Bartimaeus' response encourages us to be bold and courageous in our faith. Despite the crowd's attempts to silence him, Bartimaeus boldly called out to Jesus and went to Him when called. This boldness is important for us as well. Responding to Jesus' call often requires courage and the willingness to go against the opinions or expectations of others. It means being willing to stand firm in our faith and take bold steps to follow Jesus. This courage and boldness are essential for our spiritual growth and our ability to make a positive impact in the world.

Bartimaeus' immediate response to Jesus' call also teaches us about the importance of obedience. When Jesus called him, Bartimaeus didn't hesitate or question; he simply obeyed. This obedience is crucial for us as well. Responding to Jesus' call means being willing to obey His commands and follow His guidance, even when it is difficult or inconvenient. It means trusting that Jesus knows what is best for us and being willing to follow His lead. This obedience demonstrates our faith and trust in Jesus and allows us to grow in our relationship with Him.

In addition, Bartimaeus' response shows the importance of gratitude. After receiving his sight, Bartimaeus followed Jesus, showing his gratitude for the healing he had received. In our own lives, responding to Jesus' call should be accompanied by a heart of gratitude. We should be thankful for the ways Jesus has worked in our lives and the blessings He has given us. This gratitude helps us to stay focused on Jesus and to appreciate His love and grace. It also encourages us to share our blessings with others and to live a life of generosity and kindness.

Bartimaeus' response also teaches us about the importance of community. When Jesus called him, the people around Bartimaeus encouraged him to go to Jesus. This support from the community is important for us as well. Responding to Jesus' call often involves the support and encouragement of others. Being part of a faith community provides us with the strength and encouragement we need to follow Jesus. It helps us to stay accountable and to grow in our faith. By being part of a supportive community, we can better respond to Jesus' call and live out our faith in meaningful ways.

Furthermore, Bartimaeus' response highlights the importance of hope. By calling out to Jesus and responding to His call, Bartimaeus showed his hope that Jesus could and would help him. This hope is crucial for us as well. Responding to Jesus' call involves having hope in His promises and His ability to work in our lives. It means believing that no matter what challenges we face, Jesus is there to help us and guide us. This hope gives us the strength and motivation to respond to Jesus' call and to persevere in our faith journey.

Bartimaeus' response also teaches us about the importance of faithfulness. By immediately going to Jesus when called, Bartimaeus demonstrated his faithfulness to Jesus. This faithfulness is important for us as well. Responding to Jesus' call means being faithful to Him and His teachings. It means staying committed to our faith and our relationship with Jesus, even when it is difficult. This faithfulness helps us to grow closer to Jesus and to experience His love and guidance in our lives.

In addition, Bartimaeus' response shows the importance of transformation. When he came to Jesus, Bartimaeus received his sight and experienced a profound transformation in his life. This transformation is something that we can experience as well when we respond to Jesus' call. Jesus has the power to transform our lives and to bring healing and renewal. By responding to His call, we open ourselves up to this transformation and allow Jesus to work in our lives in powerful ways.

Moreover, Bartimaeus' response teaches us about the importance of surrender. By casting aside his cloak and going to Jesus, Bartimaeus demonstrated his willingness to surrender everything to Jesus. This surrender is crucial for us as well. Responding to Jesus' call means being willing to surrender our own plans, desires, and possessions to Him. It means trusting that Jesus knows what is best for us and being willing to follow His lead. This surrender allows us to fully embrace the new life that Jesus offers and to experience His blessings and guidance.

Bartimaeus' response also highlights the importance of joy. After receiving his sight, Bartimaeus followed Jesus with joy and gratitude. This joy is something that we can experience as well when we respond to Jesus' call. Following Jesus brings joy and fulfillment because it allows us to live in alignment with God's will and to experience His love and grace. This joy motivates us to continue following Jesus and to share His love with others.

In conclusion, Bartimaeus' immediate and wholehearted response to Jesus' call teaches us many important lessons. When Jesus called him, Bartimaeus didn't hesitate; he cast aside his cloak, rose, and went to Jesus. This response shows us the importance of being prompt and wholehearted in our response to Jesus' call. It teaches us to be attentive and sensitive to Jesus' voice, to let go of anything that hinders our approach to Him, to have faith and trust in His power and goodness, to recognize our need for Him, to take action, to be ready for transformation, to embrace new beginnings, to have boldness and courage, to practice obedience, to show gratitude, to seek community support, to have hope, to remain faithful, to allow transformation, to surrender fully, and to find joy in following Jesus. By responding to Jesus' call in this way, we can grow closer to Him, experience His love and guidance, and live a life that reflects His grace and compassion. Just as Bartimaeus experienced healing and renewal by responding to Jesus, we too can experience profound transformation and blessings when we respond to Jesus' call promptly and wholeheartedly. This response is a powerful demonstration of our faith and commitment to Jesus, showing that we are willing to follow Him wherever He leads and to embrace the abundant life that He offers.

Chapter 7 – Request

When Jesus passed by, Bartimaeus began to shout out, "Jesus, Son of David, have mercy on me!" Despite the crowd's attempts to silence him, he continued to call out, showing his faith and determination. Jesus, hearing his cries, stopped and called him over. When Bartimaeus approached, Jesus asked him a direct question, "What wilt thou that I should do unto thee?" Bartimaeus didn't hesitate or offer a vague response; he clearly and specifically said, "Lord, that I might receive my sight." This direct and clear request is a powerful example of how we should approach our prayers. Bartimaeus knew exactly what he needed and was not afraid to ask for it plainly and honestly. His willingness to openly share his deepest desire with Jesus teaches us an essential lesson about being specific and honest in our prayers.

In our own prayer lives, we often approach God with vague or general requests. While it is important to pray for overall guidance and blessings, we can learn from Bartimaeus' example to be more specific about our needs and desires. Being specific in our prayers shows that we have taken the time to think deeply about what we need and that we trust God to handle even the most detailed aspects of our lives. It also demonstrates our faith that God cares about the specifics and is willing to meet us in our particular circumstances. When we clearly articulate our needs, we invite God into the details of our lives and show that we believe in His power to intervene and provide precisely what we need.

Moreover, Bartimaeus' request highlights the importance of honesty in our relationship with God. God already knows our hearts and our needs, but He desires that we come to Him openly and transparently. When Bartimaeus asked for his sight, he did so with full honesty, expressing his deepest desire without holding back. This level of honesty in prayer is crucial for us because it allows us to build a genuine relationship with God. It means not hiding our true feelings, struggles, or desires but bringing them all before God. Honest prayers reflect a deep level of trust and reliance on God, acknowledging that we depend on Him for all aspects of our lives.

Another significant aspect of Bartimaeus' request is his faith in Jesus' ability to fulfill it. By asking Jesus to restore his sight, Bartimaeus demonstrated his belief that Jesus had the power to heal him. This faith is a critical component of effective prayer. When we come to God with our requests, we should do so with the confidence that He is able to meet our needs and answer our prayers. This doesn't mean that we will always get exactly what we ask for, but it shows our trust in God's power and wisdom. Faith in God's ability to answer our prayers aligns our hearts with His will and helps us to accept His answers, whether they match our desires or lead us in a different direction.

Bartimaeus' interaction with Jesus also emphasizes the importance of persistence in prayer. He didn't give up when the crowd tried to silence him but continued to call out until Jesus responded. This persistence is a vital lesson for us. Sometimes, we might not see immediate answers to our prayers, and it can be tempting to give up. However, Bartimaeus' example teaches us to keep praying and to keep bringing our requests before God, trusting that He hears us and will respond in His perfect timing. Persistent prayer reflects a steadfast faith and a determination to remain connected to God despite any obstacles we might face.

Additionally, Bartimaeus' clear request was a moment of vulnerability. Asking for something so specific required him to be open about his deepest need and hope. In our own lives, being specific and honest in our prayers can also make us feel vulnerable. It means admitting our weaknesses, needs, and desires, and trusting that God will not only hear us but also respond with love and compassion. This vulnerability in prayer is an important part of building a strong and intimate relationship with God. It helps us to let go of our defenses and to rely fully on God's grace and provision.

Moreover, Bartimaeus' request demonstrates humility. He came before Jesus not demanding or expecting but asking humbly for mercy. This humility is crucial in our prayers. We should approach God with a humble heart, recognizing His greatness and our dependence on Him. Humility in prayer acknowledges that we are not in control and that we need God's intervention in our lives. It shows respect and reverence for God, understanding that He knows what is best for us and will provide according to His perfect will.

The story also highlights the power of Jesus' response to Bartimaeus' specific request. Jesus restored his sight, showing that He not only hears but also acts on our behalf. This response from Jesus encourages us to trust that God is attentive to our prayers and is capable of providing what we need. It reassures us that our specific requests are important to God and that He is willing to intervene in our lives in meaningful ways. This understanding can deepen our faith and encourage us to approach God with confidence and trust.

Furthermore, Bartimaeus' request led to a transformation in his life. Once his sight was restored, he was no longer a blind beggar but a man with a new opportunity for a different life. This transformation is a powerful reminder of what can happen when we bring our specific requests to God. God can bring about significant changes in our lives when we are honest and specific in our prayers. He can provide healing, guidance, and new opportunities that align with His plan for us. This potential for transformation encourages us to be bold in our prayers, knowing that God can and will work powerfully in our lives.

Bartimaeus' story also teaches us about the importance of gratitude. After receiving his sight, Bartimaeus followed Jesus, showing his gratitude for the miracle he had experienced. This response of gratitude is important for us as well. When God answers our prayers, we should respond with thankfulness, recognizing His goodness and faithfulness. Gratitude in prayer helps to keep our hearts focused on God and reminds us of His continual presence and provision in our lives. It also fosters a positive and joyful attitude, helping us to see God's blessings even in challenging times.

Additionally, Bartimaeus' request and Jesus' response illustrate the importance of personal relationship in prayer. Jesus took the time to ask Bartimaeus what he wanted, showing personal attention and care. This interaction emphasizes that our prayers are not just requests sent out into the void but are part of a personal conversation with a loving God. When we pray, we are engaging in a relationship with God who knows us intimately and cares deeply about our lives. This personal relationship is at the heart of effective prayer, making it a two-way communication where we share our hearts and listen for God's guidance and response.

The example of Bartimaeus also encourages us to be clear and direct in our prayers, avoiding vague or ambiguous requests. Clarity in prayer helps us to focus on what we truly need and to communicate that need effectively to God. It shows that we have taken the time to reflect on our situation and to identify our specific needs. This clarity can also help us to recognize God's answers to our prayers when they come, as we can see how He has addressed our specific requests.

Moreover, Bartimaeus' clear request is a testament to the power of simple, heartfelt prayer. His request was not elaborate or complicated but was a straightforward expression of his deepest need. This simplicity is a reminder that our prayers do not need to be filled with fancy words or complex phrases to be effective. What matters most is the sincerity and honesty of our hearts. Simple, heartfelt prayers are powerful because they come from a place of genuine need and trust in God's provision.

Additionally, the story of Bartimaeus encourages us to be bold in our prayers. Bartimaeus did not hold back or let fear prevent him from asking for what he truly needed. This boldness is important for us as well. We should not be afraid to bring our deepest desires and needs before God, trusting that He is capable of providing for us. Bold prayers demonstrate our confidence in God's power and our belief in His ability to work in our lives. They show that we trust God with our most significant needs and are willing to rely on His strength and wisdom.

Furthermore, Bartimaeus' request highlights the importance of persistence in prayer. Despite the crowd's attempts to silence him, Bartimaeus continued to call out to Jesus until he was heard. This persistence is crucial for us as well. Sometimes, we might not receive immediate answers to our prayers, and it can be tempting to give up. However, Bartimaeus' example teaches us to keep praying and to keep bringing our requests before God, trusting that He hears us and will respond in His perfect timing. Persistent prayer reflects a steadfast faith and a determination to remain connected to God despite any obstacles we might face.

Bartimaeus' story also emphasizes the importance of faith in our requests. By asking Jesus to restore his sight, Bartimaeus demonstrated his belief that Jesus had the power to heal him. This faith is a critical component of effective prayer. When we come to God with our requests, we should do so with the confidence that He is able to meet our needs and answer our prayers. This doesn't mean that we will always get exactly what we ask for, but it shows our trust in God's power and wisdom. Faith in God's ability to answer our prayers aligns our hearts with His will and helps us to accept His answers, whether they match our desires or lead us in a different direction.

In conclusion, the story of Bartimaeus teaches us the importance of being specific and honest in our prayers. When Jesus asked Bartimaeus what he wanted, he clearly expressed his request to receive his sight. This clear and direct request shows us the power of making specific and honest requests in our prayers to God. It encourages us to be open and transparent in our relationship with God, to have faith in His ability to meet our needs, to be persistent and bold in our prayers, to approach God with humility, and to be clear and direct in our communication with Him. By following Bartimaeus' example, we can deepen our relationship with God and experience the power of His love and provision in our lives. Just as Jesus responded to Bartimaeus' specific request, He will respond to our prayers, providing us with the guidance, support, and blessings we need to live out His purpose for our lives. This story reminds us that our prayers are a vital part of our relationship with God and that by being specific and honest in our requests, we can experience the fullness of His love and grace.

Chapter 8 – Reliance

Bartimaeus sat by the roadside, hoping for mercy, when he heard that Jesus was passing by. Despite being blind, Bartimaeus recognized that Jesus could heal him, and he began to shout, "Jesus, Son of David, have mercy on me!" The crowd tried to silence him, but Bartimaeus persisted, showing his unwavering faith. His faith was so strong that it captured Jesus' attention, and Jesus stopped and called him over. When Bartimaeus came to Jesus, he asked, "What wilt thou that I should do unto thee?" Bartimaeus replied clearly, "Lord, that I might receive my sight." Jesus then affirmed, "Go thy way; thy faith hath made thee whole." Immediately, Bartimaeus received his sight and followed Jesus. This story highlights the incredible power of relying on faith. Jesus' statement, "Thy faith hath made thee whole," underscores that Bartimaeus' healing was directly linked to his faith. This teaches us that our faith is a critical component in receiving God's healing and blessings.

Faith is more than just belief; it is complete trust and confidence in God's power and love. Bartimaeus' reliance on faith was evident in his persistence and determination. Despite the crowd's attempts to silence him, he continued to cry out to Jesus, fully believing that Jesus could heal him. This kind of reliance on faith is something we should strive to emulate in our own lives. When we face challenges, difficulties, or need healing, we must rely on our faith in God. This means trusting that God hears our prayers and has the power to answer them. It means believing that God's love and power are greater than any obstacle we face. Just as Bartimaeus' faith led to his healing, our faith can open the door for God's blessings and miracles in our lives.

Reliance on faith involves trusting God's timing and plan. Bartimaeus didn't know when or if Jesus would heal him, but he trusted enough to keep calling out. In our lives, we often face situations where we don't see immediate answers to our prayers. During these times, reliance on faith means continuing to trust God, believing that He is working behind the scenes for our good. It means being patient and steadfast, knowing that God's timing is perfect. Our faith should not waver because of delays or uncertainties. Instead, we should hold firmly to our belief in God's promises and His ability to bring about the best outcomes for us.

Moreover, Bartimaeus' story teaches us that faith requires action. His faith was not passive; it was active and persistent. He didn't just sit quietly hoping for a miracle; he actively called out to Jesus and seized the opportunity when it came. This active faith is crucial for us as well. We must be proactive in our faith, taking steps that align with our trust in God. This could mean continuing to pray fervently, seeking God's guidance in our decisions, and stepping out in faith when God calls us to take action. By actively living out our faith, we demonstrate our reliance on God's power and His plans for our lives.

Another lesson from Bartimaeus' reliance on faith is the importance of unwavering belief even in the face of opposition. The crowd around Bartimaeus tried to silence him, but he did not let their discouragement stop him from reaching out to Jesus. Similarly, in our lives, we might face naysayers or situations that challenge our faith. In these moments, we must remain steadfast and continue to rely on our faith. This unwavering belief is a testament to our trust in God and our confidence that He will come through for us. It shows that our faith is not dependent on our circumstances but on the unchanging nature of God.

Bartimaeus' story also highlights the transformative power of faith. When Jesus told him, "Thy faith hath made thee whole," it was a declaration that his faith had brought about not just physical healing but also spiritual renewal. This transformation is available to us as well when we rely on our faith. God's healing and blessings are not limited to our physical needs; they encompass our entire being. By relying on faith, we open ourselves up to the full spectrum of God's transformative power, allowing Him to heal our bodies, minds, and spirits.

Furthermore, Bartimaeus' immediate response to follow Jesus after receiving his sight demonstrates the proper response to God's blessings. When we experience God's healing and blessings through our faith, our natural response should be one of gratitude and a desire to follow Him more closely. Bartimaeus didn't just receive his sight and go his own way; he chose to follow Jesus. This shows us that reliance on faith is not just about receiving from God but also about committing our lives to Him in response to His goodness. Our faith journey is a continuous process of trusting God, receiving His blessings, and growing in our relationship with Him.

Reliance on faith also means being vulnerable and honest with God about our needs. Bartimaeus was open about his desire to receive his sight. In our own prayers, we should be specific and honest about our needs and desires, trusting that God cares deeply about every aspect of our lives. This honesty in prayer builds a deeper connection with God and shows our reliance on His ability to provide for us. By being open with God, we allow Him to work in our lives in specific and meaningful ways.

Additionally, Bartimaeus' reliance on faith was rooted in his recognition of who Jesus was. He called out to Jesus as the "Son of David," acknowledging Jesus' messianic role and His power to heal. This recognition is essential for our faith as well. Understanding who God is—His power, love, and faithfulness—strengthens our reliance on Him. When we fully grasp the nature of God, our faith becomes more robust, and we can trust Him more completely. Recognizing God's attributes and His promises gives us the confidence to rely on Him in every situation.

Bartimaeus' story also teaches us that faith can lead to unexpected blessings. He sought physical healing, but his encounter with Jesus brought about a deeper spiritual awakening and a new direction for his life. Similarly, when we rely on faith, God often provides blessings that exceed our expectations. He knows our needs better than we do and can provide abundantly more than we ask or imagine. This encourages us to trust God's plan and be open to the broader scope of His blessings in our lives.

Reliance on faith is also about surrendering control to God. Bartimaeus' faith meant letting go of his own ability to change his situation and placing his trust entirely in Jesus. In our lives, reliance on faith requires us to surrender our control and trust God's sovereignty. It means believing that God is in control and that His plans are good, even when we don't understand them. Surrendering to God allows us to experience His peace and assurance, knowing that He is working all things for our good.

Moreover, Bartimaeus' reliance on faith resulted in a testimony that glorified God. His healing was a public demonstration of God's power and mercy. When we rely on faith and experience God's blessings, it creates a testimony that can inspire and encourage others. Sharing our stories of God's faithfulness and provision can strengthen the faith of those around us and bring glory to God. Our testimonies become powerful tools for witnessing and spreading the message of God's love and power.

The story of Bartimaeus also encourages us to approach God with boldness and confidence. His persistent calls to Jesus showed that he was not afraid to approach the Savior with his needs. This boldness is important for us as well. We should approach God's throne of grace with confidence, knowing that He is a loving Father who desires to hear and answer our prayers. This boldness in prayer is a reflection of our reliance on God's character and His promises.

Bartimaeus' reliance on faith also teaches us about the importance of recognizing and seizing the opportunities that God places before us. When Jesus passed by, Bartimaeus did not let the moment slip away; he seized the opportunity to call out for healing. In our lives, God often presents us with opportunities to exercise our faith and receive His blessings. We need to be attentive and responsive to these moments, trusting that God is opening doors for us. Seizing these opportunities demonstrates our reliance on God's timing and His provision.

Furthermore, Bartimaeus' story illustrates that faith often requires perseverance. Despite the crowd's attempts to silence him, Bartimaeus persisted in calling out to Jesus. This perseverance is a crucial aspect of reliance on faith. In our faith journey, we may face challenges, doubts, and discouragements, but we must continue to persevere. Trusting in God's promises and holding on to our faith, even in difficult times, shows our steadfast reliance on Him.

The healing of Bartimaeus also underscores the communal aspect of faith. The crowd, initially a barrier, eventually became the medium through which Bartimaeus was brought to Jesus. This transformation of the crowd's role shows that our faith journey is often intertwined with others. We rely on our faith community for support, encouragement, and sometimes even for facilitating our encounters with God. Being part of a faith community strengthens our reliance on God as we share our experiences and build each other's faith.

Reliance on faith is not just a one-time event but a continuous journey. Bartimaeus' faith led to his healing, but his decision to follow Jesus afterward shows that his reliance on faith was ongoing. In our lives, reliance on faith should be a daily practice. It means continually trusting God in all circumstances, seeking His guidance, and relying on His strength. This ongoing reliance on faith keeps us grounded in our relationship with God and allows us to experience His presence and power daily.

Additionally, Bartimaeus' story reminds us that reliance on faith often involves taking risks. By calling out to Jesus, Bartimaeus risked ridicule and rejection from the
crowd. In our faith journey, relying on God may require us to step out of our comfort zones and take risks for His sake. This could mean

standing up for our beliefs, making difficult decisions, or trusting God in uncertain situations. Taking these risks demonstrates our reliance on God's protection and provision.

Moreover, the transformation in Bartimaeus' life shows that reliance on faith leads to a deeper connection with Jesus. After receiving his sight, Bartimaeus chose to follow Jesus, signifying a new path and purpose in his life. This deeper connection is a natural outcome of relying on faith. As we trust God and experience His work in our lives, our relationship with Him deepens, and we are drawn closer to His heart. This deeper connection brings fulfillment and joy, knowing that we are walking in alignment with God's will.

Bartimaeus' healing also emphasizes the holistic nature of God's blessings. His faith not only restored his physical sight but also transformed his entire life. This holistic blessing is a reminder that God's healing and provision encompass every aspect of our lives—physical, emotional, spiritual, and relational. When we rely on faith, we open ourselves to the full scope of God's blessings, allowing Him to work in every area of our lives.

Furthermore, Bartimaeus' reliance on faith highlights the importance of gratitude. After his healing, Bartimaeus followed Jesus, likely filled with gratitude for the miracle he experienced. Gratitude is an essential response to God's blessings. It keeps our hearts humble and reminds us of God's goodness. Expressing gratitude for God's work in our lives strengthens our reliance on Him and keeps us focused on His continual provision and grace.

In conclusion, the story of Bartimaeus is a powerful testament to the importance of reliance on faith. His unwavering belief in Jesus' power to heal him, despite the obstacles he faced, led to a miraculous transformation in his life. Jesus' affirmation, "Thy faith hath made thee whole," underscores the critical role that faith plays in receiving God's healing and blessings. Bartimaeus' story teaches us to trust in God's timing and plan, to be proactive and persistent in our faith, to have unwavering belief even in the face of opposition, and to recognize the transformative power of faith. It also encourages us to respond to God's blessings with gratitude, to build a deeper connection with Jesus through our faith, and to take risks for the sake of our faith. By following Bartimaeus' example, we can strengthen our reliance on God and experience the fullness of His healing and blessings in our lives. Just as Bartimaeus' faith led to his physical and spiritual healing, our reliance on faith can lead to profound transformations and abundant blessings in our own lives. This reliance on faith is a continuous journey, one that draws us closer to God and allows us to experience His love, grace, and power in every aspect of our lives. Through unwavering faith and trust in God's promises, we can navigate the challenges of life with confidence, knowing that God is always with us, ready to heal, provide, and guide us on our journey.

Chapter 9 – Reverence

The story of Bartimaeus, a blind beggar from Jericho, as described in Mark 10:46-52, illustrates the profound impact of recognizing and revering Jesus. Bartimaeus, sitting by the roadside, heard that Jesus of Nazareth was passing by and began to shout, "Jesus, Son of David, have mercy on me!" Despite the crowd's attempts to silence him, he persisted, demonstrating his faith and desperation. Jesus heard his cries, stopped, and called him over. When Bartimaeus approached, Jesus asked him what he wanted, and Bartimaeus replied, "Lord, that I might receive my sight." Jesus then said, "Go thy way; thy faith hath made thee whole." Immediately, Bartimaeus received his sight and chose to follow Jesus along the road. This act of following Jesus after being healed is a powerful demonstration of reverence and gratitude. Reverence, in this context, means deep respect and honor for Jesus, recognizing Him as Lord and Savior, and living in a way that reflects this respect. Bartimaeus' immediate decision to follow Jesus shows that he not only sought physical healing but also acknowledged Jesus' authority and responded with a commitment to discipleship. This reverence is an essential aspect of the Christian life, calling us to live in continuous acknowledgment of Jesus' lordship and to serve Him faithfully.

Living a life of reverence involves recognizing the blessings we receive from Jesus and responding with a heart of gratitude and devotion. Bartimaeus' story teaches us that when we experience God's goodness, our response should be to honor Him with our lives. This means making a conscious decision to follow Jesus daily, just as Bartimaeus did. It requires us to prioritize our relationship with Jesus above all else, seeking to grow closer to Him through prayer, reading the Bible, and participating in the life of the church. By doing so, we demonstrate our reverence for Jesus and our commitment to living according to His teachings.

Moreover, reverence for Jesus involves obedience to His commands. After receiving his sight, Bartimaeus didn't just go back to his old life; he chose to follow Jesus, indicating his willingness to obey and live under Jesus' guidance. In our own lives, reverence means aligning our actions and decisions with Jesus' teachings. It means living in a way that reflects our faith and commitment to Him, even when it is challenging. Obedience is a crucial aspect of reverence because it shows that we respect Jesus' authority and trust His wisdom. By obeying Jesus, we honor Him and acknowledge His rightful place as Lord of our lives.

Additionally, living a life of reverence means serving Jesus and others. Bartimaeus' decision to follow Jesus likely involved serving alongside Him and helping to spread His message. In our lives, reverence is expressed through acts of service, both within the church and in our communities. Serving others in Jesus' name is a way to show our gratitude for the blessings we have received and to share His love with those around us. This service can take many forms, such as volunteering, helping those in need, and using our talents and resources to further God's kingdom. By serving others, we reflect Jesus' love and demonstrate our reverence for Him.

Reverence also involves worship. Bartimaeus' act of following Jesus can be seen as a form of worship, acknowledging Jesus' power and expressing gratitude for His healing. Worship is a vital part of living a life of reverence, as it allows us to express our love and admiration for Jesus. Worship can take many forms, including singing, praying, and participating in communion. It is an opportunity to focus our hearts and minds on Jesus, to thank Him for His blessings, and to seek His presence in our lives. Regular worship helps us to maintain a posture of reverence and keeps our relationship with Jesus at the center of our lives.

Furthermore, reverence for Jesus involves humility. Bartimaeus approached Jesus with humility, recognizing his need for mercy and healing. This humility is essential for us as well. Living a life of reverence means acknowledging our dependence on Jesus and recognizing that we cannot live according to His will without His help. Humility allows us to submit to Jesus' authority and to seek His guidance in all aspects of our lives. It also helps us to stay grounded and to avoid the pride that can hinder our relationship with Jesus. By approaching Jesus with humility, we demonstrate our reverence for Him and our willingness to follow His lead.

Living a life of reverence also means being thankful. Bartimaeus' decision to follow Jesus after receiving his sight shows his gratitude for the miracle he experienced. In our own lives, we should cultivate an attitude of thankfulness, recognizing the many blessings we receive from Jesus. Gratitude helps us to stay focused on the positive aspects of our lives and to appreciate God's continuous work in and around us. By regularly expressing our thanks to Jesus, we acknowledge His goodness and demonstrate our reverence for Him.

Moreover, reverence involves trusting Jesus completely. Bartimaeus showed great trust in Jesus' ability to heal him, and this trust was a key part of his faith. In our own lives, reverence means placing our trust in Jesus, believing in His power and goodness, even when we face challenges. Trusting Jesus allows us to experience His peace and assurance, knowing that He is in control and that His plans for us are good. This trust is a vital aspect of our relationship with Jesus and helps us to maintain a posture of reverence in all circumstances.

Additionally, living a life of reverence means sharing our faith with others. Bartimaeus' healing and subsequent decision to follow Jesus likely served as a powerful testimony to those around him. In the same way, we are called to share the story of how Jesus has worked in our lives, bringing healing and transformation. By sharing our testimonies, we honor Jesus and help others to see His power and love. Evangelism is an important aspect of reverence, as it spreads the message of Jesus and invites others to experience His blessings. By being open about our faith and sharing it with others, we demonstrate our reverence for Jesus and our commitment to His mission.

Reverence also involves making sacrifices. Bartimaeus left behind his old life, including his cloak, to follow Jesus. This act of leaving behind his past is symbolic of the sacrifices we are sometimes called to make in our own lives. Living a life of reverence means being willing to give up anything that hinders our relationship with Jesus or our ability to serve Him fully. This could involve making difficult choices, such as changing our lifestyle, letting go of certain habits, or even re-evaluating relationships. Sacrifices made for the sake of following Jesus demonstrate our deep respect and commitment to Him.

Furthermore, reverence for Jesus means being consistent in our faith. Bartimaeus' decision to follow Jesus wasn't just a one-time event; it was a continuous commitment. In our own lives, we must strive to be consistent in our faith, following Jesus every day, not just when it is convenient or easy. This consistency helps us to grow in our relationship with Jesus and to live out our faith in meaningful ways. By being consistent in our devotion to Jesus, we show our reverence for Him and our dedication to His teachings.

Additionally, living a life of reverence involves seeking to know Jesus more deeply. Bartimaeus' decision to follow Jesus suggests a desire to learn from Him and to be close to Him. In our own lives, we should seek to know Jesus more intimately through studying the Bible, prayer, and spending time in His presence. This deepening relationship helps us to understand His will for our lives and to grow in our faith. By continually seeking to know Jesus better, we demonstrate our reverence for Him and our desire to live according to His guidance.

Reverence also involves being joyful. Bartimaeus' healing likely brought him great joy, and this joy was expressed in his decision to follow Jesus. In our own lives, living a life of reverence means embracing the joy that comes from knowing Jesus and experiencing His blessings. This joy should be evident in our attitudes and actions, reflecting the gratitude and love we have for Jesus. By living joyfully, we honor Jesus and show others the impact of His presence in our lives.

Moreover, living a life of reverence means being hopeful. Bartimaeus' faith and healing filled him with hope for a better future. In our own lives, reverence involves holding on to the hope that Jesus offers, even in difficult times. This hope gives us the strength to persevere and to trust in Jesus' promises. By maintaining a hopeful attitude, we demonstrate our reverence for Jesus and our confidence in His faithfulness.

Furthermore, reverence involves being committed to spiritual growth. Bartimaeus' decision to follow Jesus indicates a desire to grow in his faith and understanding. In our own lives, we should prioritize our spiritual growth, seeking to become more like Jesus in our thoughts, words, and actions. This commitment to growth helps us to deepen our relationship with Jesus and to live out our faith more fully. By continually striving to grow spiritually, we demonstrate our reverence for Jesus and our dedication to His teachings.

Additionally, living a life of reverence means being resilient. Bartimaeus faced obstacles in his pursuit of Jesus, but he persisted. In our own lives, we will encounter challenges and setbacks, but reverence means remaining steadfast in our faith and commitment to Jesus. This resilience helps us to navigate difficulties with grace and trust in Jesus' guidance. By being resilient in our faith, we show our reverence for Jesus and our confidence in His power.

Reverence also involves being peaceful. Bartimaeus' healing likely brought him a sense of peace, knowing that his faith had been rewarded. In our own lives, living a life of reverence means embracing the peace that comes from knowing Jesus and trusting in His care. This peace should be evident in our interactions with others, reflecting the calm and assurance we have in Jesus. By

living peacefully, we honor Jesus and show others the impact of His presence in our lives.

Furthermore, living a life of reverence means being forgiving. Jesus' teachings emphasize the importance of forgiveness, and reverence for Him involves following this command. In our own lives, we should strive to forgive others as Jesus has forgiven us. This forgiveness demonstrates our respect for Jesus' teachings and helps to maintain healthy, loving relationships. By being forgiving, we show our reverence for Jesus and our commitment to living according to His will.

Additionally, reverence involves being loving. Bartimaeus' story is ultimately a story of love—Jesus' love for him and his response of love and devotion to Jesus. In our own lives, living a life of reverence means embodying this love in all that we do. It means loving God with all our heart, soul, mind, and strength, and loving our neighbors as ourselves. This love is the foundation of our faith and should be evident in our actions and attitudes. By living lovingly, we honor Jesus and reflect His love to the world.

Moreover, living a life of reverence means being faithful. Bartimaeus' faith was a key part of his healing, and his decision to follow Jesus shows his continued faithfulness. In our own lives, we should strive to be faithful to Jesus in all that we do, trusting in His promises and following His guidance. This faithfulness is a testament to our reverence for Jesus and our commitment to His teachings. By being faithful, we show our respect and honor for Jesus and our dedication to living according to His will.

In conclusion, the story of Bartimaeus is a powerful example of the importance of reverence for Jesus. After being healed, Bartimaeus chose to follow Jesus, demonstrating his deep respect and gratitude. This act of following Jesus is a model for us, showing that living a life of reverence involves recognizing the blessings we receive from Jesus and responding with a heart of gratitude and devotion. It means prioritizing our relationship with Jesus, obeying His commands, serving others, worshiping regularly, approaching Him with humility, being thankful, trusting Him completely, sharing our faith, making sacrifices, being consistent, seeking to know Him more deeply, embracing joy and hope, committing to spiritual growth, being resilient, peaceful, forgiving, loving, and faithful. By following Bartimaeus' example, we can live lives that honor Jesus and reflect our deep reverence for Him. This reverence is not just about acknowledging Jesus as Lord and Savior but about living in a way that shows our commitment to Him every day. It is about recognizing the transformative power of His love and grace in our lives and responding with unwavering devotion and gratitude. Through reverence, we can deepen our relationship with Jesus, experience the fullness of His blessings, and share His love with the world.

Chapter 10 – Recount

Bartimaeus, sitting by the roadside in Jericho, heard that Jesus was passing by and began to shout, "Jesus, Son of David, have mercy on me!" Despite the crowd's attempts to silence him, Bartimaeus persisted, demonstrating his unwavering faith and desperation for healing. Jesus, moved by Bartimaeus' faith, stopped and called him over. When Bartimaeus approached, Jesus asked him what he wanted, and Bartimaeus replied, "Lord, that I might receive my sight." Jesus then said, "Go thy way; thy faith hath made thee whole." Immediately, Bartimaeus received his sight and chose to follow Jesus along the road. This miraculous healing did not just transform Bartimaeus' life but also served as a powerful testimony to those who witnessed it. The recounting of this miracle likely spread quickly, encouraging others to seek Jesus and trust in His power to heal and transform lives. Bartimaeus' healing stands as a reminder of the importance of sharing our testimonies of God's work in our lives, as these stories have the power to inspire faith and trust in others.

When we recount our testimonies of God's work in our lives, we are sharing the evidence of His love, power, and faithfulness. Just as Bartimaeus' healing was a visible and powerful demonstration of Jesus' miracles, our own stories of God's intervention in our lives can serve as proof of His active presence in the world. Sharing our testimonies helps to build faith in those who hear them, encouraging them to seek and trust in God. It reminds others that God is not distant or inactive but is deeply involved in our lives, working for our good and His glory.

Recounting our testimonies also serves to glorify God. When we share the ways in which God has worked in our lives, we are giving Him the credit and honor He deserves. It is a way of acknowledging that our successes, healings, and transformations are not due to our own efforts but are the result of God's grace and power. This act of glorifying God through our testimonies can inspire others to praise and worship Him as well, creating a ripple effect of faith and gratitude.

Moreover, sharing our testimonies can provide hope and encouragement to those who are struggling. Just as the recounting of Bartimaeus' healing would have given hope to other blind or suffering individuals, our stories of God's faithfulness can offer comfort and encouragement to those who are facing difficulties. Hearing about how God has worked in our lives can remind others that they are not alone and that God is able and willing to help them as well. It can strengthen their faith and give them the courage to keep trusting God, even in the midst of trials.

Recounting our testimonies also strengthens our own faith. As we reflect on the ways in which God has intervened in our lives, we are reminded of His goodness and faithfulness. This reflection can deepen our gratitude and reinforce our trust in God. It helps us to see the bigger picture of God's work in our lives and to recognize His hand in both the big and small events. This practice of recounting God's work can become a source of strength and encouragement for us, especially during challenging times.

Additionally, sharing our testimonies fosters a sense of community and connection among believers. When we share our stories of God's work in our lives, we are opening up and being vulnerable with others, which can create deeper bonds and mutual support. It encourages others to share their own testimonies, creating a culture of openness and faith-sharing. This communal recounting of God's work can strengthen the faith of the entire community, as believers are reminded of God's presence and power in their collective lives.

Recounting our testimonies also serves as a form of evangelism. Just as Bartimaeus' healing would have been a powerful witness to non-believers, our stories of God's work can introduce others to the reality of His presence and power. Sharing our testimonies with those who do not yet know Jesus can be a gentle and personal way to share the gospel. It shows that our faith is not just theoretical but is based on real, tangible experiences of God's love and power. This personal witness can be a powerful tool in drawing others to seek and trust in God.

Furthermore, recounting our testimonies helps to keep our focus on God and His work in our lives. In the busyness of everyday life, it can be easy to forget or overlook the ways in which God has been faithful to us. By regularly recounting and sharing our testimonies, we keep God's work at the forefront of our minds. This practice helps us to maintain a posture of gratitude and dependence on God, reminding us of His continual presence and provision.

Sharing our testimonies also helps to build a legacy of faith for future generations. Just as the story of Bartimaeus has been passed down through the generations, our testimonies can be shared with our children, grandchildren, and beyond. These stories can become part of our family's faith heritage, providing a foundation of faith and trust in God for future generations. They serve as a reminder of God's faithfulness across the ages and can inspire faith and trust in those who come after us.

Recounting our testimonies also aligns with biblical teachings. Throughout the Bible, we see examples of God's people recounting His mighty works and miracles. The Psalms are filled with recountings of God's faithfulness and acts of deliverance. In the New Testament, the apostles often recounted the miracles and teachings of Jesus. This practice of recounting God's work is an integral part of the biblical narrative and serves as a model for us to follow. By sharing our testimonies, we are participating in this rich tradition of faith-sharing and bearing witness to God's work.

Moreover, sharing our testimonies can be an act of obedience to God's command to be His witnesses. In Acts 1:8, Jesus tells His disciples, "You will be my witnesses in Jerusalem, and in all Judea and Samaria, and to the ends of the earth." Part of being a witness involves sharing what we have seen and experienced of God's work in our lives. By recounting our testimonies, we are fulfilling this command and helping to spread the message of God's love and power.

Additionally, recounting our testimonies can inspire others to seek their own encounters with God. Hearing about how God has worked in our lives can motivate others to seek Him more earnestly and to trust Him more fully. It can encourage them to pray more, read the Bible more, and look for ways in which God is working in their own lives. This inspiration can lead to a deeper and more vibrant faith for those who hear our testimonies.

Furthermore, sharing our testimonies can help to dispel doubts and build faith in others. Just as Bartimaeus' healing would have served as a powerful evidence of Jesus' power, our testimonies can provide tangible proof of God's presence and action. Hearing real-life stories of God's work can help to strengthen the faith of those who may be struggling with doubt or unbelief. It reminds them that God is real, active, and involved in our lives.

Recounting our testimonies also helps to keep our hearts focused on God's goodness. When we take the time to reflect on and share the ways in which God has blessed us, it helps to cultivate a heart of gratitude and worship. It keeps us mindful of God's continuous work in our lives and helps us to remain thankful for His many blessings. This gratitude can transform our outlook on life, making us more positive and hopeful.

Moreover, sharing our testimonies can provide comfort and encouragement to those who are going through similar struggles. Just as Bartimaeus' healing would have given hope to others who were suffering, our testimonies can offer comfort to those who are facing similar challenges. It reminds them that they are not alone and that God is able to bring healing and deliverance. This comfort and encouragement can be a powerful source of strength for those who are in need.

Additionally, recounting our testimonies can help to build a culture of faith and expectation within our communities. When we regularly share stories of God's work, it creates an atmosphere of faith and anticipation. It reminds everyone that God is at work and encourages them to look for His hand in their own lives. This culture of faith can lead to greater prayerfulness, trust, and expectancy within the community.

Furthermore, sharing our testimonies can help to break down barriers and build connections with others. Personal stories of God's work can resonate with people on a deep level and help to build bridges of understanding and empathy. It shows that we are all on a journey of faith and that we can support and encourage each other along the way. These connections can strengthen our relationships and build a sense of unity and fellowship.

Recounting our testimonies also serves as a reminder of God's faithfulness over time. Reflecting on the ways in which God has worked in our lives helps us to see His faithfulness throughout different seasons and circumstances. It reminds us that God has been with us in the past and will continue to be with us in the future. This reminder of God's faithfulness can provide great comfort and assurance, especially during times of uncertainty or difficulty.

Moreover, sharing our testimonies can help to inspire action and change. Hearing about how God has worked in someone's life can motivate others to take steps of faith, make positive changes, or seek God's guidance in their own lives. It can inspire them to pursue their own relationship with God more intentionally and to look for ways to serve and honor Him. This inspiration can lead to meaningful and lasting transformation in their lives.

Additionally, recounting our testimonies helps to keep the memory of God's work alive. Just as the story of Bartimaeus has been passed down through the generations, our testimonies can be shared and remembered, preserving the memory of God's faithfulness. This preservation of memory

helps to build a rich tapestry of faith history that can inspire and encourage future generations. It serves as a testament to God's unchanging nature and His continual work in the world.

Furthermore, sharing our testimonies can help to combat discouragement and doubt in our own lives. Reflecting on and recounting the ways in which God has been faithful to us in the past can provide a source of encouragement and strength when we face new challenges. It reminds us of God's goodness and His ability to bring us through difficult situations. This reflection can bolster our faith and help us to remain steadfast in our trust in God.

Moreover, recounting our testimonies can bring glory to God by highlighting His attributes and character. When we share stories of God's work, we are shining a light on His goodness, love, power, and faithfulness. This glorification of God through our testimonies helps to exalt Him and to point others to His greatness. It reminds us and those who hear our stories of the incredible nature of our God and His worthiness of our praise and worship.

Additionally, sharing our testimonies can foster a sense of gratitude and contentment in our own lives. By regularly reflecting on and recounting God's blessings, we become more aware of His continuous provision and care. This awareness helps us to cultivate a heart of gratitude and to remain content in God's goodness. It shifts our focus from what we lack to the abundance of God's blessings, fostering a sense of joy and fulfillment.

Furthermore, recounting our testimonies can serve as a witness to God's transformative power. Just as Bartimaeus' healing was a visible demonstration of Jesus' miracles, our testimonies can show the world how God has transformed our lives. This witness can inspire others to seek their own transformation through a relationship with God. It highlights the life-changing impact of faith and encourages others to pursue their own journey of faith and transformation.

Moreover, sharing our testimonies can help to build a legacy of faith for future generations. Our stories of God's work can be passed down to our children and grandchildren, creating a rich heritage of faith. This legacy can inspire future generations to trust in God and to seek His guidance in their own lives. It serves as a reminder of God's faithfulness across the ages and helps to build a foundation of faith for those who come after us.

Additionally, recounting our testimonies can help to build our own faith as we reflect on God's continuous work in our lives. By regularly recounting and sharing our stories of God's intervention, we become more aware of His presence and activity. This awareness strengthens our faith and helps us to remain connected to God in all circumstances. It reminds us of His goodness and faithfulness, providing a source of encouragement and strength.

In conclusion, the story of Bartimaeus serves as a powerful reminder of the importance of recounting our testimonies of God's work in our lives. His healing not only transformed his own life but also served as a powerful witness to those around him. Similarly, when we share our testimonies, we are sharing the evidence of God's love, power, and faithfulness. Recounting our testimonies glorifies God, encourages others, provides hope and comfort, strengthens our own faith, fosters a sense of community, serves as a form of evangelism, keeps our focus on God, builds a legacy of faith, aligns with biblical teachings, fulfills our role as witnesses, inspires others, dispels doubts, offers comfort and encouragement, builds a culture of faith, breaks down barriers, preserves the memory of God's work, combats discouragement, brings glory to God, fosters gratitude and contentment, witnesses God's transformative power, and builds our own faith. By following Bartimaeus' example and sharing our testimonies, we can inspire faith and trust in others, honor God, and experience the fullness of His blessings in our lives. This practice of recounting God's work is a powerful tool for building faith, fostering community, and spreading the message of God's love and power.

Chapter 11 – Restoration

When he heard that Jesus of Nazareth was passing by, he cried out, "Jesus, Son of David, have mercy on me!" Despite the crowd's attempts to silence him, Bartimaeus persisted, demonstrating his faith and desperation. Jesus, moved by Bartimaeus' cries, stopped and called him over. When Bartimaeus approached, Jesus asked, "What do you want me to do for you?" Bartimaeus replied, "Lord, I want to see." Jesus said to him, "Go your way; your faith has made you well." Immediately, Bartimaeus received his sight and followed Jesus along the road. This miraculous restoration did not just heal Bartimaeus' physical blindness but also restored his dignity and place in society. His story highlights the compassionate nature of Jesus and His willingness to reach out to those who are marginalized, offering them hope, healing, and a new beginning. This narrative serves as a reminder of the importance of extending God's love and restoration to those who are marginalized in our own communities, offering them compassion, support, and a chance to experience God's transformative power.

In our daily lives, we encounter many individuals who are marginalized, whether due to physical disabilities, economic hardships, social stigmas, or other circumstances. Just as Jesus reached out to Bartimaeus, we are called to extend God's love and restoration to those around us who are in need. This means seeing beyond their circumstances and recognizing their inherent worth as individuals created in God's image. By offering compassion and support, we can help restore their dignity and provide them with the hope and encouragement they need to move forward.

One of the key aspects of extending God's love and restoration is showing compassion. Jesus demonstrated deep compassion for Bartimaeus by stopping and addressing his needs despite the crowd's attempts to dismiss him. In our own lives, showing compassion means taking the time to listen to and understand the struggles of those who are marginalized. It involves empathizing with their pain and offering a helping hand without judgment. Compassion moves us to action, prompting us to find ways to alleviate their suffering and provide practical assistance.

Additionally, extending God's love and restoration involves advocating for those who are marginalized. Bartimaeus' persistent cries for help were a form of self-advocacy, but it was Jesus' response that ultimately led to his restoration. In our communities, there are many who may not have the ability or opportunity to advocate for themselves. As followers of Jesus, we can use our voices and resources to stand up for their rights and needs. Advocacy can take many forms, from supporting policies that promote social justice to volunteering with organizations that provide services to those in need. By advocating for the marginalized, we help create a society where everyone has the opportunity to thrive.

Another important aspect of extending God's love and restoration is providing practical support. Jesus not only listened to Bartimaeus' request but also took action to meet his needs by restoring his sight. Similarly, we are called to provide tangible support to those who are marginalized. This could involve offering financial assistance, providing access to healthcare, helping with job training, or simply being present and offering a listening ear. Practical support helps to address the immediate needs of individuals while also empowering them to work towards long-term solutions.

Furthermore, extending God's love and restoration requires us to build inclusive communities. Bartimaeus' restoration allowed him to rejoin society and follow Jesus along the road, highlighting the importance of inclusion. In our own communities, we should strive to create environments where everyone feels welcomed and valued, regardless of their background or circumstances. This means breaking down barriers that exclude or stigmatize individuals and fostering a culture of acceptance and support. Inclusive communities reflect God's kingdom, where all are loved and valued.

Extending God's love and restoration also involves recognizing and addressing systemic issues that contribute to marginalization. While individual acts of compassion and support are crucial, we must also look at the broader systems and structures that perpetuate inequality and injustice. This requires us to engage in efforts to promote social justice and work towards systemic change. By addressing the root causes of marginalization, we can help create a more just and equitable society where everyone has the opportunity to experience God's restoration.

Additionally, extending God's love and restoration means offering spiritual support. Bartimaeus' encounter with Jesus was not just a physical healing but also a spiritual transformation. As we reach out to those who are marginalized, we should also seek to address their spiritual needs. This involves sharing the message of God's love and salvation, offering prayer and encouragement, and helping individuals to grow in their faith. Spiritual support provides individuals with the hope and strength they need to overcome their challenges and experience God's transformative power in their lives.

Moreover, extending God's love and restoration involves being persistent and patient. Just as Bartimaeus did not give up despite the crowd's attempts to silence him, we must remain committed to supporting those who are marginalized, even when it is challenging or takes time. Persistence and patience are essential qualities in our efforts to bring about restoration, as change often does not happen overnight. By staying committed and continually offering support, we demonstrate God's unwavering love and faithfulness.

Another important aspect of extending God's love and restoration is fostering empowerment. Jesus' healing of Bartimaeus empowered him to regain his independence and follow Jesus. In our efforts to support those who are marginalized, we should seek to empower them by providing opportunities for education, skill-building, and personal development. Empowerment helps individuals to regain control of their lives and work towards their goals, fostering a sense of dignity and self-worth.

Furthermore, extending God's love and restoration involves practicing humility. Jesus, the Son of God, took the time to stop and help a blind beggar, demonstrating humility and servanthood. In our own lives, we must approach our efforts to support the marginalized with humility, recognizing that we are all equal in God's eyes and that our role is to serve others with love and respect. Humility allows us to build genuine relationships and to see the value and potential in every individual.

Additionally, extending God's love and restoration means being proactive. Jesus did not wait for Bartimaeus to come to Him; He actively responded to Bartimaeus' cries for help. Similarly, we should be proactive in seeking out and addressing the needs of those who are marginalized. This involves being aware of the issues in our communities, reaching out to those in need, and taking initiative to offer support. Proactive efforts demonstrate our commitment to living out God's love and compassion.

Extending God's love and restoration also involves fostering a sense of belonging. Bartimaeus' restoration allowed him to follow Jesus and be part of the community. In our efforts to support those who are marginalized, we should seek to create spaces where individuals feel they belong and are valued. This could involve creating support groups, mentoring programs, or community events that bring people together and build meaningful connections. A sense of belonging helps individuals to feel supported and encourages them to thrive.

Furthermore, extending God's love and restoration requires us to be flexible and adaptable. Each individual's needs and circumstances are unique, and our approach to offering support should be tailored to meet those specific needs. This requires us to be open to different methods and strategies, and to be willing to adjust our efforts as necessary. Flexibility and adaptability help us to provide the most effective support and to respond to changing situations.

Additionally, extending God's love and restoration involves being a source of encouragement. Bartimaeus' encounter with Jesus likely gave him a renewed sense of hope and purpose. In our efforts to support those who are marginalized, we should strive to be sources of encouragement, offering words of hope and affirmation. Encouragement helps to uplift individuals and provides them with the motivation to keep moving forward, even in the face of challenges.

Extending God's love and restoration also means celebrating successes and milestones. When Bartimaeus received his sight, it was a moment of joy and celebration. Similarly, we should celebrate the achievements and progress of those we support, no matter how small. Celebrating successes helps to build confidence and reinforces the value of the individual's efforts. It also creates a positive and supportive environment that fosters continued growth and development.

Moreover, extending God's love and restoration involves being consistent and reliable. Bartimaeus' healing was a result of Jesus' consistent and reliable character. In our own efforts, we must strive to be consistent and reliable sources of support for those who are marginalized. This means being there for individuals when they need us, following through on our commitments, and building trust through our actions. Consistency and reliability help to create a stable foundation for individuals to build upon and to experience lasting restoration.

Additionally, extending God's love and restoration requires us to be informed and educated about the issues facing those who are marginalized. Understanding the complexities and root causes of marginalization allows us to offer more effective and compassionate support. This involves educating ourselves about social issues, listening to the experiences of those who are marginalized, and seeking out resources and training to better equip ourselves to help. Being informed and educated enables us to be more empathetic and effective in our efforts to extend God's love and restoration.

Furthermore, extending God's love and restoration involves being a positive influence. Bartimaeus' story likely inspired those around him and served as a testament to Jesus' power and compassion. In our own lives, we should strive to be positive influences, modeling God's love and compassion in our interactions with others. By living out our faith and demonstrating God's love through our actions, we can inspire others to seek and trust in God.

Moreover, extending God's love and restoration involves fostering a sense of hope. Bartimaeus' healing gave him hope for a new future. In our efforts to support those who are marginalized, we should seek to instill hope, reminding individuals of their inherent worth and potential. Hope is a powerful force that can motivate individuals to overcome

challenges and pursue their goals. By offering hope, we help to restore individuals' belief in themselves and in the possibilities for their future.

Additionally, extending God's love and restoration involves being patient and understanding. Bartimaeus' persistence was met with Jesus' patient and understanding response. In our efforts to support those who are marginalized, we must approach individuals with patience and understanding, recognizing that healing and restoration take time. Patience allows us to build trust and to offer consistent support, while understanding helps us to empathize with individuals' experiences and challenges.

Extending God's love and restoration also involves being inclusive. Jesus' healing of Bartimaeus was an inclusive act that welcomed him back into the community. In our efforts to support those who are marginalized, we should strive to create inclusive environments where everyone feels welcomed and valued. Inclusion involves recognizing and celebrating diversity, and creating spaces where individuals can fully participate and contribute. Inclusive environments reflect God's kingdom, where all are loved and valued.

Furthermore, extending God's love and restoration involves being generous. Jesus' healing of Bartimaeus was a generous act of compassion. In our own lives, we should strive to be generous with our time, resources, and support for those who are marginalized. Generosity reflects God's abundant love and provision, and it allows us to be channels of His blessings to others. By being generous, we demonstrate our commitment to living out God's love and compassion.

Moreover, extending God's love and restoration involves being faithful. Jesus' faithfulness to His mission of healing and restoration was evident in His response to Bartimaeus. In our own efforts, we must remain faithful to our calling to support those who are marginalized. This means staying committed to our efforts, even when it is challenging, and trusting in God's guidance and provision. Faithfulness helps us to persevere and to continue offering support, knowing that our efforts are part of God's greater plan for restoration.

Additionally, extending God's love and restoration involves being joyful. Bartimaeus' healing likely brought great joy to him and those around him. In our efforts to support those who are marginalized, we should strive to bring joy and positivity into their lives. Joy is a powerful force that can uplift and inspire individuals, and it reflects the love and hope that God offers. By being joyful, we create a positive and encouraging environment that fosters restoration and growth.

Extending God's love and restoration also involves being authentic. Bartimaeus' encounter with Jesus was marked by genuine faith and honesty. In our efforts to support those who are marginalized, we should strive to be authentic in our interactions, offering genuine care and support. Authenticity helps to build trust and meaningful relationships, and it allows us to connect with individuals on a deeper level. By being authentic, we demonstrate God's genuine love and compassion.

Furthermore, extending God's love and restoration involves being resilient. Bartimaeus' persistence and faith demonstrated resilience in the face of challenges. In our efforts to support those who are marginalized, we must remain resilient, continuing to offer support and care even when faced with difficulties. Resilience helps us to navigate challenges and to remain committed to our mission of restoration. By being resilient, we demonstrate our trust in God's strength and provision.

Moreover, extending God's love and restoration involves being kind. Jesus' interaction with Bartimaeus was marked by kindness and compassion. In our efforts to support those who are marginalized, we should strive to be kind in our words and actions. Kindness reflects God's love and care, and it has the power to uplift and encourage individuals. By being kind, we create a supportive and nurturing environment that fosters restoration and growth.

Additionally, extending God's love and restoration involves being hopeful. Bartimaeus' healing was a testament to the hope that Jesus offers. In our efforts to support those who are marginalized, we should strive to instill hope, reminding individuals of God's promises and the potential for a better future. Hope is a powerful motivator that can inspire individuals to overcome challenges and pursue their goals. By being hopeful, we demonstrate our trust in God's faithfulness and His ability to bring about restoration.

In conclusion, the story of Bartimaeus is a powerful example of God's care for the marginalized and the transformative power of His restoration. Bartimaeus' healing by Jesus not only restored his physical sight but also his dignity and place in society. This narrative serves as a reminder of the importance of extending God's love and restoration to those who are marginalized in our own communities. By offering compassion, support, advocacy, practical assistance, inclusion, empowerment, humility, proactivity, belonging, flexibility, encouragement, celebration, consistency, education, positivity, hope, patience, understanding, generosity, faithfulness, joy, authenticity, resilience, kindness, and hope, we can help restore the dignity and potential of those who are marginalized. This practice of extending God's love and restoration is a powerful tool for building faith, fostering community, and spreading the message of God's love and power. By following Jesus' example and reaching out to those in need, we can be instruments of God's healing and restoration, bringing hope and transformation to individuals and communities.

Chapter 12 - Repentance:

The story of Bartimaeus, a blind beggar from Jericho, as recorded in Mark 10:46-52, provides a profound lesson about the importance of repentance and recognizing our need for Jesus. Bartimaeus sat by the roadside, marginalized by his blindness and reduced to begging for his survival. When he heard that Jesus of Nazareth was passing by, he began to shout, "Jesus, Son of David, have mercy on me!" Despite the crowd's attempts to silence him, Bartimaeus persisted, crying out even louder. His plea for mercy was not just a request for physical healing but also a reflection of a heart of repentance, recognizing his deep need for Jesus' intervention in his life. Jesus, moved by Bartimaeus' faith and repentance, stopped and called him over. When Bartimaeus approached, Jesus asked him, "What do you want me to do for you?" Bartimaeus replied, "Lord, I want to see." Jesus said to him, "Go your way; your faith has made you well." Immediately, Bartimaeus received his sight and followed Jesus along the road. This miraculous encounter highlights the transformative power of repentance and faith, showing that when we recognize our need for Jesus and call out to Him with a repentant heart, He responds with mercy, healing, and restoration. This narrative teaches us the vital importance of maintaining a heart of repentance in our own lives, continually turning to Jesus and seeking His mercy.

Repentance is a fundamental aspect of the Christian faith, involving a sincere recognition of our sins and a genuine turning away from them. Bartimaeus' call for mercy exemplifies this attitude. By crying out to Jesus, he acknowledged his own helplessness and his need for divine intervention. In our lives, maintaining a heart of repentance means regularly examining ourselves, acknowledging our shortcomings, and seeking Jesus' forgiveness and guidance. It involves a humble recognition that we cannot navigate life on our own and that we need Jesus' grace and mercy to overcome our weaknesses and sins.

This continuous turning to Jesus keeps our hearts aligned with His will and open to His transformative work.

One of the key elements of repentance is humility. Bartimaeus' willingness to publicly cry out for mercy, despite the scorn of the crowd, demonstrates true humility. He was not concerned about his dignity or the opinions of others; his focus was solely on reaching Jesus. In our own lives, we must adopt a similar posture of humility, recognizing that we are all sinners in need of God's grace. This humility allows us to approach Jesus honestly and openly, without pretense or pride. By humbling ourselves before Jesus, we create space for His mercy to enter our lives and bring about genuine transformation.

Moreover, Bartimaeus' persistence in seeking Jesus' mercy highlights the importance of perseverance in repentance. Despite the crowd's attempts to silence him, Bartimaeus continued to cry out until he was heard. This perseverance is crucial in our own journey of repentance. There will be times when we face discouragement, opposition, or feel overwhelmed by our sins, but we must continue to seek Jesus' mercy with unwavering determination. Perseverance in repentance demonstrates our sincere desire for change and our trust in Jesus' ability to bring about that change in our lives.

Maintaining a heart of repentance also involves a sincere desire for transformation. Bartimaeus did not just want to receive his sight; he wanted to follow Jesus and live a new life. His healing was both physical and spiritual, reflecting a complete transformation. In our own lives, repentance should lead to a genuine desire to change our ways and live according to Jesus' teachings. It means not just seeking forgiveness for past sins but also committing to a new path of righteousness and obedience to God's will. This desire for transformation is a sign of true repentance and a heart that is open to Jesus' guidance.

Furthermore, Bartimaeus' call for mercy is a reminder of the importance of seeking Jesus' mercy regularly. Just as Bartimaeus persistently called out to Jesus, we too must continually seek His mercy in our lives. This involves regular prayer, confession, and a constant reliance on Jesus' grace. By making repentance a regular practice, we keep our hearts attuned to God's will and maintain a close relationship with Him. This continual seeking of mercy helps us to stay humble, aware of our need for Jesus, and open to His transformative work in our lives.

Additionally, Bartimaeus' story teaches us about the power of faith in the process of repentance. Jesus acknowledged Bartimaeus' faith as the key to his healing, saying, "Your faith has made you well." True repentance is intertwined with faith; it involves believing in Jesus' power to forgive, heal, and transform us. In our own lives, repentance should be accompanied by a strong faith in Jesus' ability to bring about change. This faith gives us the confidence to approach Jesus with our sins and weaknesses, trusting that He will respond with mercy and grace.

Bartimaeus' encounter with Jesus also highlights the importance of responding to Jesus' call. When Jesus called Bartimaeus, he immediately threw aside his cloak, sprang up, and went to Jesus. This response demonstrates a willingness to leave behind his old life and embrace the new life that Jesus offered. In our own lives, repentance involves a similar response. When we hear Jesus' call, we must be willing to leave behind our old ways, habits, and sins, and step into the new life that He offers. This response requires courage and a genuine commitment to follow Jesus, just as Bartimaeus did.

Furthermore, the story of Bartimaeus shows us that repentance is not just about personal transformation but also about a public declaration of our faith. By crying out to Jesus in front of the crowd, Bartimaeus made a public declaration of his faith and his need for Jesus. In our own lives, repentance should involve a willingness to publicly acknowledge our faith and our need for Jesus. This public declaration serves as a testimony to others and can inspire them to seek Jesus and His mercy as well. It also reinforces our commitment to live according to Jesus' teachings and to be accountable to our faith community.

Maintaining a heart of repentance also means being open to the guidance of the Holy Spirit. The Holy Spirit convicts us of our sins and leads us towards repentance. By being sensitive to the Holy Spirit's prompting, we can recognize areas in our lives that need change and seek Jesus' forgiveness and guidance. This openness to the Holy Spirit helps us to continually grow in our faith and to live in alignment with God's will.

Moreover, Bartimaeus' story reminds us of the joy and freedom that come from repentance. After receiving his sight, Bartimaeus followed Jesus along the road, experiencing a new sense of purpose and direction. In our own lives, true repentance brings about a sense of joy and freedom as we are released from the burden of our sins and experience the transforming power of Jesus' grace. This joy and freedom motivate us to continue living in a state of repentance, continually seeking Jesus' mercy and striving to live according to His will.

Furthermore, maintaining a heart of repentance involves practicing forgiveness towards others. Just as we seek Jesus' mercy and forgiveness, we are called to extend that same mercy and forgiveness to those who have wronged us. This practice of forgiveness reflects the heart of repentance and helps to cultivate a spirit of grace and compassion in our relationships. By forgiving others, we demonstrate our understanding of the mercy we have received from Jesus and our commitment to living out His teachings in our daily lives.

Additionally, Bartimaeus' story highlights the importance of gratitude in the process of repentance. After receiving his sight, Bartimaeus followed Jesus, likely filled with gratitude for the miracle he had experienced. In our own lives, repentance should be accompanied by a heart of gratitude for Jesus' mercy and grace. This gratitude helps us to remain humble and to recognize the ongoing work of Jesus in our lives. By regularly expressing our thanks to Jesus, we keep our focus on

His goodness and maintain a heart that is open to His transformative power.

Maintaining a heart of repentance also involves being part of a faith community. Bartimaeus' healing took place in the context of a community, with witnesses who saw and likely shared his story. In our own lives, being part of a faith community provides support, encouragement, and accountability as we seek to live in a state of repentance. Our faith community can help us to stay focused on Jesus, offer guidance and prayer, and celebrate our growth and transformation. By being actively involved in a faith community, we can strengthen our commitment to repentance and experience the collective support of fellow believers.

Moreover, the story of Bartimaeus teaches us that repentance is an ongoing process. Just as Bartimaeus' healing marked the beginning of a new journey with Jesus, our repentance is not a one-time event but a continuous journey of growth and transformation. Maintaining a heart of repentance means continually turning to Jesus, seeking His mercy, and striving to live according to His teachings. This ongoing process helps us to remain aligned with God's will and to experience the continual work of His grace in our lives.

Furthermore, maintaining a heart of repentance involves being intentional in our spiritual practices. Regular prayer, reading the Bible, and participating in worship are essential practices that help us to stay focused on Jesus and to cultivate a repentant heart. These practices provide opportunities for self-examination, confession, and renewal, helping us to stay connected to Jesus and to continually seek His mercy. By being intentional in our spiritual practices, we create space for Jesus to work in our lives and to bring about lasting transformation.

Additionally, maintaining a heart of repentance means being willing to receive correction and guidance from others. Just as Bartimaeus received direction from Jesus, we must be open to receiving feedback and guidance from trusted individuals in our faith community. This willingness to receive correction helps us to stay humble and to recognize areas in our lives that need change. By being open to the insights and encouragement of others, we can grow in our faith and deepen our commitment to repentance.

Moreover, the story of Bartimaeus highlights the importance of responding to Jesus' call with immediacy. When Jesus called him, Bartimaeus immediately threw aside his cloak and went to Jesus. In our own lives, when we sense Jesus calling us to repentance, we should respond without delay. This immediacy reflects our sincerity and urgency in seeking Jesus' mercy and transformation. By responding promptly to Jesus' call, we demonstrate our commitment to living a life of repentance and our desire to align ourselves with His will.

Furthermore, maintaining a heart of repentance involves being mindful of our thoughts and actions. Bartimaeus' desire to see was both a physical and spiritual longing. In our own lives, we must be mindful of our thoughts and actions, striving to live in a way that reflects our commitment to Jesus. This mindfulness helps us to recognize when we fall short and to seek Jesus' forgiveness and guidance. By being intentional in our daily lives, we can cultivate a heart of repentance and stay focused on our journey of faith.

Additionally, the story of Bartimaeus teaches us about the power of testimony. Bartimaeus' healing and subsequent following of Jesus served as a powerful testimony to those around him. In our own lives, sharing our stories of repentance and transformation can inspire and encourage others. By being open about our journey and the ways in which Jesus has worked in our lives, we can provide hope and encouragement to those who may be struggling. Our testimonies serve as a reminder of Jesus' mercy and the transformative power of repentance.

Maintaining a heart of repentance also involves recognizing the ongoing need for God's grace. Bartimaeus' call for mercy was a recognition of his dependence on Jesus. In our own lives, we must continually acknowledge our need for God's grace and mercy. This recognition keeps us humble and reliant on Jesus, knowing that we cannot navigate life on our own. By continually seeking God's grace, we remain open to His work in our lives and experience the ongoing transformation that comes from living in a state of repentance.

Moreover, maintaining a heart of repentance involves seeking reconciliation. Just as Bartimaeus' healing restored his place in the community, our repentance should lead us to seek reconciliation in our relationships. This involves making amends for past wrongs, seeking forgiveness, and working towards healing and restoration. Reconciliation reflects the heart of repentance and helps to build stronger, healthier relationships. By seeking reconciliation, we demonstrate our commitment to living out Jesus' teachings and fostering a spirit of unity and love.

In conclusion, the story of Bartimaeus provides a powerful lesson on the importance of maintaining a heart of repentance. His call for mercy reflects a genuine recognition of his need for Jesus and a desire for transformation. In our own lives, we must continually turn to Jesus, seeking His mercy and grace. This involves humility, perseverance, a desire for transformation, regular prayer and confession, faith, a public declaration of our faith, openness to the Holy Spirit, joy and freedom, forgiveness, gratitude, being part of a faith community, ongoing self-examination, intentional spiritual practices, receiving correction, immediacy in responding to Jesus' call, mindfulness, sharing our testimony, recognizing our need for God's grace, and seeking reconciliation. By maintaining a heart of repentance, we align ourselves with God's will, experience His transformative power, and live out our faith in a way that honors Jesus and inspires others. This ongoing journey of repentance keeps our hearts attuned to God's work in our lives and allows us to continually grow in our relationship with Him. Just as Bartimaeus experienced restoration and transformation through his encounter with Jesus, we too can experience the fullness of God's mercy and grace as we maintain a heart of repentance and continually seek His presence in our lives.

Conclusion

As we conclude "The Shout That Stopped The Saviour," the story of Blind Bartimaeus from Mark 10 serves as a powerful reminder of the transformative power of faith and the compassionate response of Jesus to those who seek Him earnestly. Bartimaeus' encounter with Jesus is not just a historical event; it is a timeless lesson that continues to resonate with us today, offering profound insights into the nature of faith, the importance of persistence, and the incredible love and mercy of Christ.

Bartimaeus' shout was more than just a cry for physical healing; it was a declaration of faith, a recognition that Jesus was the Messiah, the Son of David, who had the power to change his life. In a world that often tries to silence our voices, to diminish our cries for help, Bartimaeus' story encourages us to persist in our faith, to boldly approach Jesus with our needs, and to trust that He hears us, even in the midst of the noise and chaos of life.

The fact that Jesus stopped for Bartimaeus, despite the urgency of His journey and the pressing crowd, reveals a profound truth about the character of God. Jesus is never too busy, never too preoccupied, to hear the cry of a sincere heart. He is attentive to the needs of those who call out to Him, regardless of their status or circumstances. This story reassures us that our cries for help, our prayers of desperation, do not go unnoticed. When we call out to Jesus, we can be confident that He hears us and that He is ready to respond with grace, mercy, and power.

Bartimaeus' healing was not just about receiving physical sight; it was a complete transformation. His faith in Jesus led to a new life, one where he could see clearly, follow Jesus, and live out his days as a testimony to the power of God. This story challenges us to consider what we are seeking from Jesus. Are we content with temporary relief, or are we longing for a deeper, more transformative encounter with Him? Bartimaeus didn't just ask for his sight; he asked for mercy, recognizing that what he needed most was not just physical healing, but the compassionate touch of the Saviour who could restore his entire being.

In reflecting on Bartimaeus' story, we are reminded that faith is not passive; it is active, persistent, and bold. It is a faith that cries out to Jesus, even when others try to silence us. It is a faith that believes in His power to change our lives and that trusts in His timing and His ways. And most importantly, it is a faith that is met with the love and compassion of Jesus, who stops, listens, and responds to our deepest needs.

"The Shout That Stopped The Saviour" invites us to embrace this kind of faith in our own lives. It encourages us to cry out to Jesus with boldness, to trust in His response, and to follow Him with the same dedication that Bartimaeus showed. May this story inspire us to live lives marked by persistent faith, knowing that the same Jesus who stopped for Bartimaeus is ready to stop for us, to listen to our cries, and to lead us into a life transformed by His grace.

Don't miss out!

Visit the website below and you can sign up to receive emails whenever Joshua Rhoades publishes a new book. There's no charge and no obligation.

https://books2read.com/r/B-A-AJLBB-SLBYE

BOOKS 2 READ

Connecting independent readers to independent writers.

Did you love *The Shout That Stopped The Saviour*? Then you should read *Renewed Hope- How to Find Encouragement in God*[1] by Joshua Rhoades!

[2]

In a world where challenges and hardships seem to come at us from every side, it's easy to feel overwhelmed, discouraged, and even hopeless. We all face moments when we wonder how we will ever make it through the difficulties we encounter. But in these times, the Bible offers us a powerful example of finding strength and hope, no matter the circumstances. In 1 Samuel 30:6, we read about David, a man who faced great trials and overwhelming odds, yet in the midst of it all, "David encouraged himself in the LORD his God." This simple yet profound statement serves as the foundation for this book, "Renewed Hope- How to Find Encouragement in God." David's life was filled with ups and downs, moments of triumph and times of deep despair. He knew what it was like to be pursued by enemies, to experience loss, and to feel abandoned. Yet, even in his darkest hours, David found a way to renew his hope by turning to God. He didn't rely on his own strength or seek comfort in worldly solutions. Instead, he looked to the LORD, drawing strength and encouragement from his relationship

---

1. https://books2read.com/u/boeko1

2. https://books2read.com/u/boeko1

with God. This book is an invitation to explore how we, too, can find renewed hope and encouragement in God, just as David did. It is a guide to understanding the power of faith, prayer, and trusting in God's promises, even when life seems unbearable. Throughout these pages, we will explore practical ways to draw closer to God, to encourage ourselves in Him, and to discover the peace and strength that come from relying on the LORD. Whether you are facing a specific challenge right now or simply want to deepen your relationship with God, this book will provide you with the tools and inspiration you need to find encouragement in the LORD. As we journey together through the principles found in David's example, you will learn how to shift your focus from the problems that surround you to the God who sustains you. You will discover that no matter what life throws at you, there is always hope in the LORD, and by encouraging yourself in Him, you can face any situation with renewed strength and confidence. This is not just a book about surviving difficult times, but about thriving through them by finding your hope and encouragement in the unchanging character of God. So, whether you are struggling with personal challenges, feeling weighed down by the burdens of life, or simply seeking a deeper sense of peace and purpose, "Renewed Hope-How to Find Encouragement in God" is here to remind you that you are not alone, and that with God, there is always a reason to hope. Let David's example inspire you to turn to the LORD, to find your strength in Him, and to walk forward with a renewed sense of hope, no matter what you face.